MATERIALS·

ARIZONA'S ENERGY FUTURE

Making the Transition to a New Mix

CONTRIBUTORS

Roger L. Caldwell
Hanna J. Cortner
Gregory A. Daneke
Rocco A. Fazzolare
Helmut J. Frank
Larry A. Goldstone
Jimmye S. Hillman

Carl N. Hodges
Jack D. Johnson
Lawrence D. Mann
Edgar J. McCullough, Jr.
Michael Rieber
Robert L. Seale
Terry Triffet

ARIZONA'S ENERGY FUTURE

Making the Transition to a New Mix

Helmut J. Frank, Editor

THE UNIVERSITY OF ARIZONA PRESS
Tucson, Arizona

In Collaboration With The Arizona Academy

About the Editor...
HELMUT J. FRANK began his research into energy matters in 1950, when he joined a consulting firm specializing in the analysis of energy problems. He has since been a consultant and research associate with a number of industrial and scholarly organizations, and from 1975 to 1976 was a member of the Citizens Energy Task Force of Arizona. He has written a number of articles and books, among them *Arizona Energy Inventory,* was a contributing author to *Arizona Energy: A Framework for Decision* (University of Arizona Press), and since 1979 has been the editor of *The Energy Journal.* Dr. Frank, who received his Ph.D. in economics from Columbia University, has been a member of the faculty of the University of Arizona since 1961.

THE UNIVERSITY OF ARIZONA PRESS

This book was set in 10/11 V-I-P Baskerville
Manufactured in the U.S.A.

Library of Congress Cataloging in Publication Data
Main entry under title:

Arizona's energy future.

  Bibliography: p.
  Includes index.
  1. Energy consumption—Arizona. 2. Energy industries—Arizona. 3. Energy policy—Arizona. I. Frank, Helmut Jack, 1922–   .
HD9502.U53A645   333.79′09791   82-6941
                                      AACR2
  ISBN 0-8165-0773-2

Contents

Illustrations

A Word From the Editor

Much has been learned since the mid-1970s, by specialists as well as the general public, about the complex and sometimes frustrating problem of energy. We have learned that the energy problem is long-term and not a short-term "crisis" that will pass quickly; that there are no quick and easy solutions to the problem; that costs and tradeoffs must be faced at every turn; that government controls over supplies and prices impede rather than assist in solving the problem; that consumers and suppliers will respond to economic incentives, although often slowly and imperfectly.

This study takes a fresh look at Arizona's energy future in light of the knowledge that has been gained since 1976, when *Arizona Energy: A Framework for Decision* (University of Arizona Press) was published. It differs from the earlier study in at least two major respects. One is its emphasis on those areas which promise to make the greatest contribution to overcoming the energy problem in Arizona—conservation, cogeneration, and renewable energy sources (solar, geothermal, and biomass). It says little about established energy sources such as oil, gas, coal, hydroelectric, and nuclear, which were discussed in the 1976 volume.

The other departure is the basic approach to the subject. The previous study, in line with conventional treatment, followed disciplinary lines: technology was examined by engineers, resources by geoscientists and other specialists in the natural sciences, institutions and policies by political scientists. Each group studied a single aspect of the subject in isolation from the others. This volume, in turn, attempts to integrate all of the disciplines relevant to a topic and to bring knowledge from various fields to bear on a single subject. The participants were organized into multidisciplinary working groups, task forces, and review committees in an effort to produce a study that would reflect the integrated thinking of the participants as a whole.

This approach required greater time and effort than the usual single-discipline enquiry. Team members felt that they had gained much in the process. It is hoped that the reader will find the results equally worthwhile.

HELMUT J. FRANK

Acknowledgments

The editor and contributors wish to express their appreciation to the Arizona Academy, sponsor of the Arizona Town Hall, which requested the preparation of the report on which this book is based, and which suggested numerous editorial improvements; the Arizona Energy Office, a division of the Governor's Office of Economic Planning and Development, for financial assistance and substantive comments; the Arizona Solar Energy Commission, for reviewing drafts of Chapter 5; Mervin L. Brown, Arizona Public Service Company, for contributing material to Chapter 5; and to the following individuals, for their help in preparing this book: Edwin H. Carpenter, Dennis C. Cory, Tres English, Reid H. Ewing, William R. Fasse, Peter F. Ffolliot, Dixon T. Gaines III, Wilford R. Gardner, P. Kenneth Godwin, Donna R. Iams, Helen J. Kessler, John O. Kessler, R. Larry Medlin, George V. Mignon, Louis N. Nelson, Thomas F. Saarinen, Raymond A. Sierka, Stephen E. Smith, Claudia Stone, James C. Wade, Donald H. White, Donovan C. Wilkin, and Robert H. Wortman. Numerous research assistants, secretaries, librarians, and other support staff helped in the many tasks involved in the preparation of this study; we also thank them. Thanks are due to the University of Arizona Press for effecting publication of this volume.

Part I

The Setting

Chapter 1

Arizona: The State and Its Resources

Arizona is 1,742 miles from Chicago and 2,415 miles from New York City. Most Americans' impressions of the state are not derived from personal contact, but from television series and magazine advertisements. Not surprisingly, these sources are neither complete nor well balanced. To understand the state's energy position and problems, it is necessary to have a grasp of some basic, generally unrecognized facts.

Although in terms of size Arizona is the sixth-largest state, it ranks only twenty-ninth in population (2.7 million on July 1, 1980 [1980 census]). This gives a density of twenty-four people per square mile, much sparser than the overall U.S. density of sixty-one. Interestingly enough, Arizona's population is slightly more urbanized than the U.S. as a whole; 75 percent of Arizonans live in the two major metropolitan areas of Phoenix and Tucson, while only 73 percent of Americans live in metropolitan areas. However, Arizona's cities are very large in size: on July 1, 1981, Phoenix had an area of 331 square miles, and Tucson, 102 square miles.

The state is about one-third mountainous and two-thirds steppe or desert. Elevation of cities ranges from 138 feet above sea level in Yuma to nearly 7,000 feet in Flagstaff. The climate thus exhibits great variations, although it is generally much drier than the eastern and midwestern United States. Flagstaff's temperature ranges are similar to those found in Chicago. Most of the population, however, lives in low desert areas where summers are hot (average July temperature range is 78–105°F) and winters mild (January range: 38–65°F). Sunshine is abundant; Phoenix gets 86 percent possible sunshine, compared to 36 percent in Chicago. The mild winters and springs attract many retirees and tourists. The hot summers produce high seasonal energy and water demands, i.e., air conditioners and swimming pools.

Arizona's natural beauty draws visitors from around the world. In addition to the Grand Canyon, prime attractions range from the picturesque Indian lands in the north to the cactus deserts in the south. The state's cultural and historical heritage draws from twenty-two Indian tribal groups, Mexico, and the English-speaking cowboys and settlers.

In many parts of Arizona, one can see for a hundred miles on a clear day. That pristine air quality is being threatened by smog and smelter pollution, particularly in the big cities and the Four Corners areas. Concern for environmental quality has led Arizona to place pollution controls on coal and copper plants. It is one of the few states to require an annual emissions inspection for late model automobile registration in the metropolitan counties.

Arizona's mineral deposits include non-ferrous metals and coal. Coal is found on the Navajo Indian Reservation; only a small fraction of total deposits was under lease and being mined as of 1981. Arizona's copper production, which amounted to 66 percent of total U.S. production in 1979, has earned it the title "Copper State." Molybdenum is another important mineral produced in Arizona mines.

Farming is another vital activity; cattle, cotton, and feed crops head the list of cash earners. Limited water, however, is a serious constraint on agriculture—and threatens to impede urban and industrial growth in some areas as well. Crop usage is only 2 percent of the state's total area. Average annual rainfall is 7 inches in the Phoenix area and only 2.7 inches in Yuma, so that farming is heavily dependent on irrigation.

Total water consumption for all uses in 1970 was 4.8 million acre feet, of which 2.5 million came from groundwater. The natural recharge rate of groundwater was only 300,000 acre feet per year, leaving an overdraft of 2.2 million acre feet; thus, the groundwater supply is being depleted, especially in Tucson, the largest city in the world entirely dependent on groundwater. The Central Arizona Project, now under construction, is a massive aqueduct and reservoir system designed to bring Colorado River water to Phoenix and Tucson. However, even the CAP is expected to solve Tucson's water problems only temporarily. It is clear that agriculture, which once accounted for 89 percent of total water consumption, will continue to decrease as an economic factor.

If one wanted to characterize Arizona in one word, it would be "growth." Arizona is one of the fastest-growing states in the nation. From 1970 to 1980, total personal income grew 262 percent, ranking the state third behind Wyoming and Nevada.

Population grew 53 percent, making Arizona second, behind Nevada, and wage and salary employment grew by 83 percent, placing it third behind Nevada and Wyoming. Personal income per capita, $8,791 in 1980, was slightly (2 percent) below the U.S. average, but the gap has been narrowing. Employment is dominated by light industries and services. Trade accounted for 23 percent of the total in 1980, services for 20 percent, and government for 20 percent. Manufacturing, about 15 percent, is primarily light and clean: electronics, laboratories and aircraft. It is characterized by new plants with low energy use. Electronics firms have been especially attracted to the Phoenix area and to Tucson.

Arizona is a dynamic state, politically conservative, venturesome in business, positive in outlook. The energy problems of the 1970s came as a shock, but the reaction has been wholesome. The questions most frequently asked are: What are our alternatives to oil and gas? How can we learn to use what we have in abundance? What do we need to do to get on with the job? Even if there are no definitive answers as yet, the positive outlook represented by such questions holds promise for the future.

Energy Demand Characteristics

Because of its low concentration of high energy-consuming industries, Arizona's direct per capita annual energy consumption is somewhat lower than the national average (330 million versus 359 million Btus in 1979). It also differs in its composition. Arizona's industrial energy consumption is significantly below the national average (29 percent of total energy usage versus 40 percent nationally).* On the other hand, the low population density, great distances between localities, absence of strong mass transit systems, and large number of tourists cause the transportation sector to be unusually large—34 percent of total consumption against 25 percent nationally (see Fig. 1.1).

Arizonans continue to rely heavily on the scarcest sources—petroleum and natural gas—for satisfying their energy needs. The combined share of these fuels in 1979 was 68 percent of total energy consumption (Fig. 1.2). The large role of oil reflects the dominance of the transportation sector, which accounts for 70 percent of total petroleum usage. In addition, some major industrial users and power plants were forced to shift from natural gas to petroleum during the mid-1970s, when their

---

*While Arizona has little indigenous heavy industry consuming large amounts of energy locally, the Arizona lifestyle is highly dependent on the products of such industries (steel, aluminum, paper, chemicals, etc.). Hence, per capita consumption of total energy by Arizonans—including the energy content of all goods consumed—is considerably higher than direct energy use only.

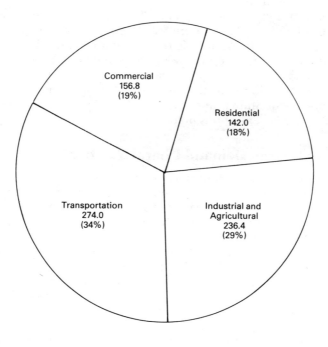

Total: 809.2 trillion Btu

Per Capita: 330 million Btu

Commercial
156.8
(19%)

Residential
142.0
(18%)

Transportation
274.0
(34%)

Industrial and
Agricultural
236.4
(29%)

Figure 1.1   *Arizona Gross Energy Consumption by End Use, 1979 (Trillion Btu)*

Source: U.S. Department of Energy.

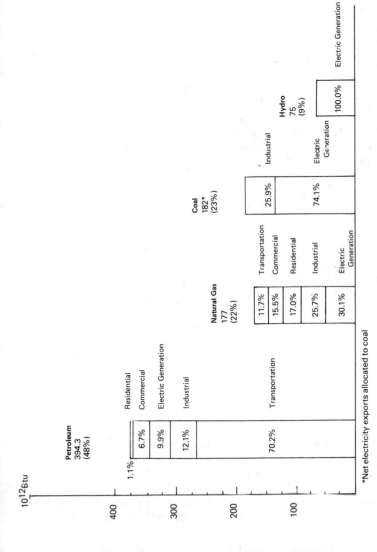

10^{12}Btu

Petroleum
394.3
(48%)

1.1% — Residential
6.7% — Commercial
9.9% — Electric Generation
12.1% — Industrial

70.2% — Transportation

Natural Gas
177
(22%)

11.7% — Transportation
15.5% — Commercial
17.0% — Residential
25.7% — Industrial
30.1% — Electric Generation

Coal
182*
(23%)

25.9% — Industrial
74.1% — Electric Generation

Hydro
75
(9%)

100.0% — Electric Generation

400
300
200
100

*Net electricity exports allocated to coal

Figure 1.2   *Arizona Gross Energy Consumption by Source and End Use, 1979 (Trillion Btu)*

Source: U.S. Department of Energy.

established gas supplies were curtailed by federal and state allocations and a temporary moratorium on all new connections
was imposed between April 1976 and September 1978. The
Natural Gas Policy Act of 1978 relieved the shortage of interstate commerce supplies while continuing to hold gas prices
below market levels. This had induced some users, e.g.,
electric generating plants with dual burners, to shift back from
oil to cheaper gas.

Natural gas has been the preferred fuel in Arizona for heating buildings and water and for a variety of industrial uses since
completion of the pipeline from Texas before World War II.
Proximity to major supply sources and prices far below those of
alternative forms, whether heating oil or electricity, gave gas a
preeminent place as long as it was freely available. During the
moratorium, builders shifted to all-electric homes, provided
with either conventional heating plus evaporative coolers or
with heat pumps. Since the end of the moratorium, heat pumps
have continued to be favored in many higher-priced residences,
especially where the humidity limits the effectiveness of evaporative cooling. Elsewhere, the combination of gas heating with
evaporative cooling or conventional central air conditioning (or,
increasingly, both) remains the preferred option.

Coal consumption in Arizona expanded rapidly during the
1970s as utilities undertook construction of large coal-fired
power plants in Arizona and adjoining states. Including net imports (imports minus exports), coal had become the second
largest energy source by 1979, surpassing natural gas. This
trend is continuing with the construction of additional coal-fired
power plants and the conversion of one plant from oil/gas to
coal. Also contributing to the growth has been a shift of some
other industrial users, e.g., cement plants, from gas to coal.

Output of hydroelectric power in Arizona depends on water
availability from the Colorado and other rivers. While annual
production fluctuates, there has been no long-term increase in
recent years. As a result, the relative share of hydropower in the
state's total energy supply has declined to less than 10 percent.

Arizona as of 1981 did not have any nuclear power plants in
operation. However, three large units were under construction
forty-five miles from Phoenix. The first of these has been
scheduled to begin operating in 1983, with others to follow in
1984 and 1986. By 1986, the electricity industry in the state will
have completed its program of minimizing reliance on oil and
natural gas, and maximizing the use of coal and nuclear power.

Conventional Energy Resources

Among conventional energy resources, Arizona has significant quantities of only coal and hydro power. It ranks fifteenth

among the fifty states in identified coal resources,* with an estimated total of 21.25 billion short tons. Most of these are located
in the Black Mesa, in the northeastern part of the state, on the
Navajo and Hopi Indian Reservations. Only a small fraction of
the total is currently under lease (to Peabody Coal Co.). It contains estimated reserves of 350 to 400 million tons. The coal is
bituminous with a heat content of 11,125 to 12,382 Btu per
pound. Deposits on the Peabody lease occur within 130 feet of
the surface and are stripmined. Large-scale mining operations
started in 1970 and expanded later in the decade with completion of additional large coal-burning electric power plants.

Only small amounts of petroleum have been discovered in
Arizona. The fields are located in the extreme northeastern
corner of the state and are geologically related to the much
larger Greater Aneth field of southern Utah. As of December
31, 1979, proved reserves of crude oil were estimated at 6.5
million barrels and natural gas reserves at 45 billion cubic feet.
Average daily production of the state's thirty-three oil wells was
about 33 barrels, for a total of 406,000 barrels in 1980. Gas wells
produced 358 billion cubic feet. Annual output has declined
steadily in recent years.

Some geologists believe that Arizona holds promise of becoming an important oil and gas producing state. The theory is that
the Overthrust Belt, which has proved highly productive in the
northern Rockies, runs through a large section of the state, in a
crescent roughly from Yuma to the southeastern border. In the
late 1970s, there occurred a sudden interest in leasing acreage;
two deep exploratory wells were drilled, but proved to be dry
holes; additional tests have been planned for 1982. It is hoped
that these will yield evidence to evaluate the prospects of significant commercial discoveries in the state.

Extensive exploration for uranium was carried on in Arizona
after World War II. At the peak, in 1957, 121 operations were in
progress, concentrated in Apache, Coconino, Gila and Navajo
counties. Production of uranium ore through 1969, which
totalled nearly three million tons containing 8,900 tons of
uranium oxide (U_3O_8), represented about 4 percent of the total
U.S. supply. Estimates of economically recoverable reserves
depend greatly on market prices, available processing facilities, and the policies of those holding the mineral rights. In
the early 1970s, when prices were low, Arizona was believed to
have only a small volume of potentially recoverable reserves.
Later in the decade, when prices had increased as much as
500 percent, exploration companies renewed their interest in
the state's uranium resources, and one major company was

---

*This figure includes, in addition to measured reserves, indicated reserves and
inferred resources.

reported to be investigating the feasibility of reopening an old mine in Coconino County. Since that time, prices have again fallen sharply because of the dim prospects for nuclear energy nationally. There is little hope that an Arizona uranium industry will revive unless the national market improves drastically.

Arizona receives its hydroelectric supplies from several federally-run reclamation projects on the Colorado River and from facilities owned by the Salt River Project and private utilities, chiefly in the Phoenix area. The existing twelve generating sites, including those on the state's western border, have a total capacity of 3,120 Mw. About 875 Mw of this total are estimated to be available to Arizona, equivalent to about 1.5 percent of total installed hydroelectric capacity in the nation. Another five sites offer conventional (i.e., base load) hydroelectric potential. However, their development is not being contemplated because of the high carrying charges of capital intensive projects under the financial conditions of the late 1970s and early 1980s plus the serious environmental problems raised by some of the projects. In addition, numerous sites have been identified as having pumped storage potential. Pumped storage is used to provide power at peak demand periods, but represents a net energy loss of about one-third because of the need to pump the water back to the upper reservoir during offpeak periods.

Energy Supplies

Because of the small size of Arizona's known oil and gas deposits, virtually all supplies of these dominant fuels must be brought into the state. Moreover, in the absence of a full-product oil refinery,* petroleum products for Arizona's use are manufactured in other states. The Southern Pacific Pipeline system carries some 90 percent of Arizona's requirements for gasoline and middle distillates. It draws on refineries in western Texas and southern New Mexico to the east and southern California to the west. Sections of the state far from the pipeline and dependent on products the line cannot carry (e.g., heavy fuel oil) are serviced by truck or rail. All natural gas supplies are carried by the El Paso Pipeline, which carries supplies to the California border, with various terminals en route.

The first large-scale user of Arizona coal was the Mohave generating plant on the Nevada side of the Colorado River. Coal is pulverized at the mine and moves through a 275-mile slurry

---

*A full-product refinery has been proposed for a location near Maricopa in Pinal County. It is to operate on Alaskan crude shipped through the Four Corners Pipeline. The plant would have a capacity of 50,000 barrels per day and is scheduled to be completed in 1984. Realization of this plant depends on the owners' obtaining access to Alaskan royalty crude.

pipeline, the only one in the country. The largest user of Arizona coal is the Navajo power plant at Page, near the Utah border, which obtains its supplies by train. All other coal-fired electric power plants in the state are supplied by rail from mines in New Mexico.

Large amounts of electricity are regularly transmitted into the state from power plants located in northwestern New Mexico and, by displacement, from Colorado, in which plants Arizona utilities share equity interests. In turn, non-Arizona utilities own shares in a number of Arizona's coal-fired plants or have contracts for part of the output of these plants. They also participate in the Palo Verde nuclear power plant, which will begin operations in 1983. More than half of this plant's output is scheduled for export to California and other adjoining states. Arizona utilities are tied into the vast grid of the Western region, which allows flexible and economical interchanges of power.

For two reasons, Arizona was more severely affected by the Arab oil embargo in the late 1973–74 than many other states. First, the state's relatively high growth rates caused fuel allocations (determined on historical base periods) to run far short of demand. Second, uncertainty over whether adequate supplies of gasoline would be available greatly reduced tourist travel and inflicted serious economic damage. During the second shortage, in 1979, Arizona fared relatively better than some other states because of modifications in the allocation formula and the timely actions of industry and state government in obtaining emergency supplies.

In recent years, the electric utility industry in Arizona has been free of serious supply problems. All the major suppliers have been in the process of shifting from oil and gas to coal-fired units, and the two largest entities—Arizona Public Service Company and Salt River Project—participate in the Palo Verde nuclear plant as well. Most of this capacity was planned many years ago, when annual demand increases were high. The owners' principal task has been to delay units not yet needed, or to find out-of-state buyers for portions of the equity or output of these plants. Arizona utilities have thus been able to make mutually advantageous arrangements with companies elsewhere, especially in California, where construction of new power plants has become nearly impossible.

Chapter 2

The Changing Energy Scene

The events of the 1970s, especially the huge price increases and interruptions of petroleum supplies, have had a great impact on the energy scene in Arizona. Both the demand and supply sides of the energy equation have been affected. Perhaps most important, there has developed a keen awareness by much of the public of energy—and other resources, especially water.

On the demand side, the large increases in energy prices that occurred, beginning in 1973, have had a strong dampening effect on the growth of energy consumption in the state. Total energy usage, which grew at an average annual rate of 6.7 percent during the period of low energy prices (1960–73), has risen at an average rate of only 2.8 percent in recent years (1973–79; see Table 2.1). This rate was lower than Arizona's population increase, so that per capita annual consumption has actually declined. The slowdown occurred in all of the end-use sectors, most markedly in transportation, which has grown by only about 2 percent annually in the most recent period. Besides cutting consumption in response to higher energy prices, travelers have at times been discouraged from long-distance driving by a fear of supply shortages. Many have shifted to air travel or to vacationing in places closer to their homes.

On the supply side, there have been major shifts in the composition of the state's energy mix. The most important of these has been the substitution of coal (and to a lesser extent oil) for natural gas by large industrial users and power plants, and of electricity for gas in residential space and water heating. Interest in renewable energy sources has also grown. An increasing number of homes are relying on wood for all or part of their space heating and others are installing solar devices, especially water heaters.

[12]

Table 2.1　*Arizona Total Energy Consumption by User Class
Selected Years, 1960–1979
(Trillion Btus)*

Year	Residential	Commercial	Industrial	Transportation	Total
1960	46.6	70.9	48.5	119.6	285.6
1965	55.3	64.2	115.3	141.7	376.5
1970	85.1	104.3	138.9	193.9	522.3
1973	120.3	134.7	182.8	242.3	680.1
1979	142.0	156.8	236.4	274.0	809.2

Average Annual Percentage Changes

Arizona

| 1960–73 | 7.6 | 5.1 | 10.7 | 5.6 | 7.5 |
| 1973–79 | 2.8 | 2.2 | 3.7 | 2.1 | 2.9 |

United States

| 1960–73 | 4.3 | 5.2 | 3.5 | 4.5 | 4.1 |
| 1973–79 | 0.3 | 0.4 | 1.1 | 1.7 | 1.0 |

Source: U.S. Department of Energy, *State Energy Data Report,* September 1981.

The U.S. Demand Outlook

There is every indication that the trend toward greater energy conservation—increased efficiency of energy use—will continue. The extent to which demand projections have been reduced for the nation as a whole since pre-embargo days is shown in forecast comparisons for the year 2000 (Table 2.2). In 1972, predictions of 160 quads or more were widely accepted as "conventional wisdom," and only a minority, representing strong advocates of alternative lifestyles, forecast that consumption in 2000 would be significantly lower. By 1974, the low scenarios of the Ford Foundation Project, which forecast consumption of 100–124 quads in 2000, were considered so extreme that they provoked a group of well-known economists, led by Professor Adelman of M.I.T., to publish a formal reply.[1] Today, by contrast, the standard "conventional wisdom" forecasts range between 90 and 100 quads; the 1980 forecast of the Energy Information Administration of the U.S. Department of Energy, 97–106 quads, is considered high;[2] and predictions of 80 quads (only slightly above the current level) are considered more and more reasonable by many energy specialists.

Table 2.2   *Trends in the Forecasts of U.S. Energy Requirements
in the Year 2000
(in Quads)*

Year of Forecast	Extremely Low ("Beyond the Pale")	Low ("Heresy")	Consensus ("Conventional Wisdom")	High ("Superstition")
1972	125 (Lovins)	140 (Sierra)	160 (AEC)	190 (FPC)
1974	100 (Ford zeg)	124 (Ford tf)	140 (ERDA)	160 (EEI)
1976	75 (Lovins)	89–95 (Von Hippel)	124 (ERDA)	140 (EEI)
1977–78	33 (Steinhart, 2050)	67–77 (NAS II)	96–101 (NAS III, AW)	124 (Lapp)

Abbreviations: Sierra = Sierra Club; AEC = Atomic Energy Commission; FPC = Federal Power Commission; Ford zeg = Ford Foundation Zero energy growth scenario; Ford tf = Ford Foundation technical fix scenario; Von Hippel = Von Hippel and Williams, Center for Environmental Studies, Princeton University; NAS II and III = The National Academy of Science Committee on Nuclear and Alternative Energy Systems (CONAES); AW = Alvin Weinberg, the Institute for Energy Analysis, Oak Ridge.
Source: U.S. Department of Energy, *Low Energy Futures for the United States,* June 1980, p. 9 (titles and matrix attributed to Amory Lovins).

At the same time, however, the divergence of views of just how much lower energy growth rates will be—or, indeed whether there may not be negative growth—continues unabated. If anything, the range of projections today is wider than it was a decade ago. This reflects the fact that the energy forecaster must operate today in a far more uncertain environment than he did in pre-crisis days. Historical experience no longer is a sure guide to the energy future. Instead, we have clearly entered a period of transition, where it is difficult to make energy demand estimates with any certainty. The standard practice of planning for the future has been to stress short-term independent events rather than to conduct coordinated long-term evaluations. But major technological, economic, and social changes have occurred, the impact of which on future energy patterns cannot be ignored.

Thus, society is in the process of undergoing important shifts, including the decentralization of both institutions and technological efforts, although there are concurrent countertrends (e.g., corporate mergers); increased interest in individual initiative and the operation of market forces, rather than governmental controls and actions; and the profound impact of long-term, world-wide inflation. These and other structural changes may be the major determinants of future energy issues—even more than technical solutions, economics, or government regulations or incentives.

In addition, there are certain physical resource limits that we may be approaching for traditional energy sources (primarily oil and gas), and there is increased uncertainty and complexity in dealing with the many interdependent sectors of society, locally as well as globally. At the very least, future oil and gas will be less plentiful and more difficult to find and produce and thus will cost more in constant dollars. It is no longer relevant to simply extrapolate past experience and make minor modifications in order to accommodate future changes. Rather, the ability to anticipate the future may require an entirely new analysis, where we first look at the future and then work back to the present to determine what changes may occur.

Finally, the state of the art of forecasting is such that there is no single method that is best for analyzing the future, and a number of approaches must be taken to provide any valid results. Individual perceptions of problems vary by location, early training and exposure to the views of others, type of employment, and opinions on quality-of-life issues. It is not uncommon to have the popular view of a specific problem differ markedly from that of the experts. Symptoms are frequently mistaken for the problem itself, and when crisis situations are relieved, large segments of the public may no longer see the underlying causes. Further, the introduction of new technologies implies that actual and perceived problems become the subject of public debate and confrontation. These considerations apply to Arizona as well as to the nation as a whole; and for this reason the forecasts presented in Chapter 3 incorporate three alternative scenarios, each resting on different assumptions and yielding different outcomes.

Future Domestic Energy Supplies

Discussion of traditional energy resources and supplies for the state must take a national, if not world-wide, approach because the energy crisis is really a crisis of liquid and gaseous fuels, which Arizona must import, not of energy generally. Moreover, the price of oil, which is determined on the world market, is the most important factor in shaping the trend of energy prices.

Proved reserves of both oil and natural gas in the United States have declined steadily for the past fifteen years, and production generally trended downward during the 1970s, though there are signs that the decline has been halted. The key policy issue is whether these unfavorable developments were caused, as some contend, by man-made constraints (e.g., government price and allocation controls, restrictions on leasing, and other environmental constraints on energy production) or whether, as others maintain, they indicate the approaching exhaustion of domestic resources. In the first case, the downtrend could be halted or even reversed by changes in policy; in the second, it might be arrested temporarily by strong financial incentives but should resume within a few years.

Federal controls over natural gas production for sale across state lines have been in effect for over twenty-five years. The Natural Gas Policy Act of 1978 extended controls to intrastate sales as well, but provided for price ceilings on new gas to be lifted by 1985. Controls over crude oil prices were imposed in 1971 and removed in 1981. There is virtually unanimous agreement among energy analysts that these controls inhibited the oil and gas industry's engaging in a maximum exploration and development effort, and also that by keeping prices below true replacement costs, the controls provided energy users with inappropriate signals for their investment and consumption decisions, e.g., not shifting to small cars. Since 1978, drilling has increased sharply, gas discoveries are up, production of both oil and gas have increased, and oil consumption has fallen dramatically. These trends are expected to continue through at least part of the 1980s.

There is also no question that the United States has vast oil resources (if one includes deposits of shale oil), and the nation's gas resources, including those contained in tight formations, Devonian shales, geopressurized zones, etc., are very large. Furthermore, the technology of producing liquids and gases from coal, with which the United States is richly endowed,[3] has been under intensive development.* Liquids and gases from one or more of these unconventional sources may begin emerging later in the 1980s and making a significant contribution to total supplies in the late 1990s. None of them, however, is easy to produce; most have major technical problems that are not yet fully resolved; several have serious environmental problems and require large amounts of water and capital, and all are relatively expensive, even compared to current OPEC-determined prices.[4] Moreover, they require major energy outlays in the construction of their product facilities and significant energy inputs into their production process. Thus their net contributions are substantially less than the energy content of the coal, shale, or

---

*The technology for producing synthetic gas from coal has existed for over a hundred years. For liquids it was the basis for fueling the German and Japanese economies in World War II. However, cost is still too high to force any market penetration without government assistance.

tar sands being processed. In the case of oil shale and tar sands these production losses cannot be avoided, but with coal, the process loss must be justified by the improved value (based on convenience, cleanness, etc.) of the synthetic liquid or gas. Therefore, while the contribution of the unconventional sources may be essential during the transition period, they cannot be counted on as the principal replacement for conventional oil and gas or as the ultimate answer to the energy problem for the rest of this century. This outlook could change, however, if serious oil supply problems develop, including price increases beyond those now anticipated.

The real problem with U.S. fossil fuels, however, is not that the country is in danger of running out of resources in the strict sense—that is unlikely to happen any time soon, even with conventional oil and gas—but that the better, i.e., most convenient, lowest-cost, and most readily available sources are becoming increasingly scarce, and that development of virtually all alternatives has run into serious economic and environmental impediments. Recent studies, whether originating with industry, government, or independent research organizations, agree broadly that the amount of oil and gas left to be discovered in the United States is limited; that production of liquids can perhaps be kept level with an increasing contribution from synthetics; but that supplies of gas, following a temporary spurt resulting from decontrol, will resume their long-term decline, even with the best of efforts.[5]

World Energy Outlook

These considerations underlie the views of the contributors to this study regarding the general energy future. Specifically, it was assumed that:

1. Conventional oil and gas production cannot sustain the growth of world energy demand but nonetheless will constitute an important factor in total energy supply for several decades. There is disagreement over just how long the present level of output can be maintained, especially within the United States, how rapid the decline will be once it sets in, and how much difference the level of prices will make to volumes supplied, i.e., how high the supply elasticities are.* But there is no doubt that the most accessible oil and gas fields were discovered long ago, that economic and environmental costs of new discoveries will be much higher than in the past, and that prices will continue to increase, perhaps dramatically.

---

*Elasticity of supply is the percentage increase in the quantity supplied due to a given percentage increase in price, with all other factors constant.

2. Prices on the demand side matter a great deal. The previously held belief in a lock-step relationship between energy usage and economic activity has been altered by the unprecedented increase in energy prices. Changes in the energy-growth relationship occur through normal evolution of technology and habit, and are stimulated by higher energy prices. Assuming that acute crises are temporary, these adjustments do not imply drastic changes in lifestyles but rather marginal, gradual adaptations in ways of going about one's business (e.g., driving the same number of miles but in a more fuel-efficient vehicle).

3. OPEC* will continue to play a dominant role in setting world energy prices, and U.S. domestic prices will follow these closely now that oil has been decontrolled and gas is scheduled to be deregulated in 1985. However, OPEC is not a monolithic cartel and its power over prices has been shown to have distinct limits. It cannot continually charge higher prices and still maintain its previous level of exports. Rising oil prices, even in the face of strong demand, will attract large investments in competing energy supplies, which will eventually set limits on OPEC oil prices. By the same token, OPEC may not be able to prevent spot (market) prices from rising at certain times, e.g., when panic buying occurs, as it did in 1979. In that event, the market will lead OPEC (contract) prices upward, not the reverse.

4. Middle East supply sources will continue to be highly vulnerable. Events could take several forms, for example, a local war, revolutions in one or more producing countries, or disputes between suppliers and importers. No one can guarantee the American public against such contingencies; in fact, a solid body of knowledgeable opinion predicts that one or more crises are almost certain to occur during the 1980s. Indeed, the swing from technical shortage in 1979 to a glut in 1981 was symptomatic of the volatility of oil markets even in relatively stable times.

5. The role of synthetics and alternative fuels will be smaller under the policies of the Reagan administration than under previous ones. Market forces will be the price determinants of what sources and what technologies will be phased in, at what time, and at what volumes. The government's role in developing substitute energy sources is not being completely eliminated, but it is being substantially reduced, as is the federal role in energy conservation.[6]

Thus, the type of energy we are most accustomed to using (oil and gas still accounted for nearly 75 percent of U.S. energy demand in 1980) is becoming relatively unreliable for any long-

*The Organization of Petroleum Exporting Countries (OPEC) has 13 members. It accounts for some 60 percent of non-Communist production and for 77 percent of proved reserves.

term future. While it is not possible to predict a specific cata-
strophic event involving oil and gas supplies, it seems reasonable
to anticipate one or more disruptions in the near future.

Implications for Arizona

The precise shape Arizona's energy future will take in the
next century is far from clear. To a large extent it is still within
the power of this generation to determine that future. What is
clear is that unless we are extraordinarily lucky and none of the
potential contingencies occurs, there will have to be changes
from the accustomed way of acting and living that will be neither
easy nor costless to achieve. In this respect, both the proponents
of continuing on the traditional energy path, and their critics
who favor a shift to "soft" technologies, have oversimplified
their cases. These changes will come, and we can either react to
them in crisis fashion or anticipate them and figure them into
our individual and collective decision making.

The prime challenge ahead is to move gradually from traditional energy resources and heavy use of oil and gas toward
sustainable energy sources and more efficient energy use. While
this transition is already under way, it is not coming easily or
rapidly. It will require a reevaluation of some long-held traditional concepts. Informed public debate concerning policies and
options can assist in easing transition difficulties.

In responding to new knowledge and choosing among alternative paths it is critical to maintain a high degree of flexibility;
otherwise, great stresses and inefficiencies may result. If we wait
too long in making critical choices, commitments to inferior options will have been made, and precious time and money wasted.
However, if we move too soon or too heavily in any one direction, we may run the risk of making the wrong choice. Many new
energy sources and technologies are still in a developing stage,
and it is too soon to select one option or to standardize one
version of any new technology for more rapid commercialization. Again, all present indications are that there is no single best
solution, and it is doubtful that one will be found in the future. It
is essential, therefore, to continue developing many options,
until those that are clearly more appropriate and economical
emerge from the vast array currently being investigated.

Through public debate of the issues, Arizona can become
better prepared to maneuver through the difficult transition
period to a new energy era. Time is critical. The decisions that
we take or fail to take now will make all the difference in the lives
of our children and grandchildren.

Part II

Future Prospects and Their Determinants

Chapter 3

The Twenty-Year Outlook

Arizona's energy outlook for the balance of the twentieth century and the principal determinants of the state's energy future may be forecast with three quite different energy demand scenarios for the year 2000. Each of these scenarios depicts a different view of the state's future economy and the lifestyles of its citizens, but should be taken only as examples; only the future itself will reveal what outcome is actually realized.

The assumptions regarding the national and international energy environment affecting Arizona have been set forth in Chapter 2. For Arizona specifically, the following economic conditions are assumed for all three scenarios (see Table 3.1):

1. Population will reach 4.67 million in 2000, as projected by the Arizona Department of Economic Security (DES) in 1981.

2. Industrial employment will continue to increase substantially faster than population, especially during the 1980s.

3. Real per capita income will rise moderately and will approach the national average by the year 2000.

4. Inflation will remain high but will gradually taper off to below 7 percent annually.

The population growth rate has been raised significantly from the previous (1979) DES estimate, although not as high as some other forecasts, e.g., the Hudson Institute's report.[1] Industrial employment rises more rapidly than total population; this would imply both a continued increase in labor force participation rates (e.g., by women) and accelerated growth of the industrial sector of the state's economy. The use of the same economic assumptions for all three scenarios represents something of an oversimplification, since employment, real income, and in-migration may be affected by the energy situation. However, the precise nature of the relationship is uncertain; for example, in case of serious energy problems, population influx into Arizona may be

Table 3.1   *Arizona Economic Projections*

	Population[a] (Thousands)	Industrial Employment[b] (Thousands)	Real Personal Income Per Capita[c]	Consumer Price Index[d] (1967 = 100)
1960	1,320	164	2,230	88.6
1970	1,792	268	3,154	116.3
1980	2,733	450	3,511	246.8
1990	3,618	572	4,378	578.2
2000	4,507	754	4,933	1121.0
Average Annual Percentage Changes				
1960–70	3.1	5.0	3.5	2.8
1970–80	4.3	5.3	1.1	7.8
1980–90	2.8	4.6	2.2	8.9
1990–2000	2.4	2.8	1.2	6.8

[a]Arizona Department of Economic Security, February 10, 1981.
[b]Ratio to total population based on DES May 1979 projections.
[c]In constant 1967 dollars. Projections assume that by the year 2000 Arizona will approach the national average as forecast by Data Resources, Inc.
[d]All-urban, U.S. average. Forecast by Data Resources, Inc.

lower because mobility is reduced, or it may be higher because more people will want to move from cold to warm climates. In any case, reliable techniques have not been fully developed for tracing the interrelationship between energy and the economy in Arizona, and even the U.S. Census Bureau's methods of estimating migration are poor.

The Rationale For More Than One Energy Future

Prior to the oil embargo of 1973–74, many estimates of future energy demand were essentially simple extrapolations from previous experience, often tied to predictions of population or Gross National Product (GNP). At that time, this was a perfectly acceptable technique, because energy demand experienced a smoothly rising trend per capita and a nearly fixed relationship to GNP. Since that time, new energy demand projections have come down markedly, with the average consumption for the year 2000 being about half what was estimated only six years ago (see Chapter 2).

Precisely how these trends are changing is very difficult to determine on the basis of our limited experience with the new energy circumstances. This applies for individual sectors as well as for the total energy system. Public utilities, for example, must by law satisfy the energy demands of their customers. Accordingly, they must estimate what that demand is likely to be sufficiently in advance to permit investment decisions to be made in the face of long lead times for construction and financing. Besides responding to changes in income and prices, energy demand in Arizona is strongly affected by migration patterns and changes in the relative mix of specific sectors of the economy. Thus, major energy-producing institutions must plan under conditions of much greater uncertainty (and hence risk) than in the past.

Given these complexities, it is unduly limiting to rely on estimates of future energy use made by single individuals or groups with narrow perspectives. Rather, it is desirable to have a broad debate among many segments of the public on alternative energy futures that appear plausible. Only in this way can the key questions be addressed in the context of whatever limitations exist. In examining future scenarios, it is important to understand what the limiting factors are, how to avoid surprise situations, where to allow for changes, and how to recognize which choices are realistic and which unrealistic. Certain key variables, such as resource availability, cost, consumer decisions, and population trends, continue to be critically important. But there are others, such as availability of agricultural land for energy production, urban land use planning, building construction codes, utilization of wastes as resources, and electronic communication, to which little attention was given when energy was plentiful and cheap, but which can no longer be neglected under conditions of increasing fuel scarcity and rising energy prices.

One issue has been a special cause of controversy in the energy debate: whether to place greater stress on demand reduction or on development of domestic supply sources. All of the antagonists—advocates of consumers' versus industry's interests, regulation versus free market, environmentalism versus supply development, and pro- versus anti-nuclear groups—seem to have attached their causes to this issue. To choose ideological sides in this debate would be self-defeating. For one thing, both supply and demand play a critical role in determining resource allocation. For another thing, it should be possible to set forth some guiding principle on which most rational debaters can generally agree, although there are bound to be dissenters.

We propose the least-cost criterion as such a principle. This means that alternative options should be carefully examined and their costs compared—both costs to the private participants and to society—and the option or options selected that will yield the greatest return for each dollar invested. Any such rule has its limitations; one must identify all the costs, and these cannot always be converted to a common base such as dollars. Future private costs may not be fully known under conditions of rapidly changing technology and economics. Social costs are often even more difficult to determine, and subjective criteria may have to be used to draw acceptable boundaries.

Evaluating a single energy alternative by itself is not a fruitful exercise, because each energy source involves tradeoffs with others and with environmental, economic, and social values. Just as it is impossible to define how safe a drug is without knowing the risks of not taking the drug, so one must analyze each situation in comparison with its alternatives. Thus, a simple and popular question such as "are you in favor of solar power or not?" merely adds to existing confusion, whereas a broader formulation like "what priority do you favor for the development of solar energy as compared to increased use of nuclear power?" lends itself to critical evaluation. The least-cost criterion is useful precisely because it forces opposing parties to look at alternatives and the tradeoffs between them.

The Three Scenarios

Based on these general assumptions, three alternatives for Arizona's energy consumption in the year 2000 have been developed. Great uncertainties face the nation's and the state's energy future, and this future can still be influenced by actions taken by private and public decision makers, now and in the next few years. Study of the differences between the three energy futures and their implications for Arizona thus holds promise of considerable payoff.

Case A. High Energy Use—No Major Crisis.

This case depicts Arizona's energy balances in 1990 and 2000 on the assumption that energy supplies will be freely available, i.e., that the world oil market will not be subject to disturbances from political or other forces, that foreign oil will be permitted to enter the United States without restraints, and that the federal government will permit market forces to determine the allocation of energy supplies. Prices are assumed to rise moderately, about 2 percent per year above the general inflation rate to $52.50 in constant 1981 dollars. No additional demand modification programs will be enacted on either the federal or state levels, but energy users will continue to adapt to price increases that have already occurred and to those assumed for the future.

Case A is comparable to the low energy price scenario for the nation of the 1980 forecast by the Energy Information Administration, U.S. Department of Energy, with world oil prices at $42 a barrel in the year 2000 (in 1979 prices) and U.S. consumption at 107 quads. It represents a level of energy consumption that falls outside the current consensus of 90–100 quads. It is highly optimistic in its assumption that no serious foreign oil supply problems will occur in the next two decades.

It should be pointed out that under these conditions, Arizona and the nation would be able to meet most of their energy requirements from conventional sources (see Table 3.2). High demand for fuels would simply increase the flow of imports, and these would respond without sharply higher world prices. Given this ample availability of fuels plus the quite moderate increase in energy prices, development of alternative fuel sources would occur rather slowly, and only the most economical new sources would carve out a niche in the energy market.

Even in this scenario Arizona energy consumption increases less rapidly, in percentage terms, than it has in the past, with some exceptions. These smaller increases are primarily caused by the transportation sector, where we have assumed continued dominance of gasoline and diesel-powered vehicles, but they apply to all other sectors as well. Total consumption reaches about 1.6 quads in the year 2000, almost double that of 1980, in Case A. The average annual rate of increase, about 3.5 percent for 20 years, is greater than the population increase used in the forecast; thus, per capita consumption increases moderately. This, however, is also the result nationally for the $42-per-barrel case in the DOE forecast.

Case B.   Intermediate Energy Use—Most Likely.

Here the optimistic outlook of Case A for world oil supplies is dropped. Instead it is assumed that oil flows will be subject to one or more serious interruptions because of wars, internal upheavals, or political disputes affecting major producing countries. Along with these would come significantly sharper price increases than in Case A. They would continue to occur as "oil shocks," rather than as gradual formula-based trends, and neither their precise magnitude nor their timing could be predicted. As a result, energy users would hold down consumption by adopting efficiency measures more rapidly and more extensively than in Case A.

Under these assumptions, national energy consumption, at 80 quads in 2000, would be 25 percent below Case A and would increase little from the current level, and per capita consumption would decline. In Arizona, total energy consumption would continue to increase because of higher-than-average growth of population and economic activity. During periods of fuel supply difficulties, motorists and other users of petroleum products would be faced with very sharp price increases, but these would be of limited duration and no compulsory measures would be

Table 3.2   *Arizona Total Energy Forecast, 1980–2000*
Case A: No Major Crisis

	Residential	Commercial	Industrial	Transportation	Total
			(Trillion Btus)		
1960[a]	31.5	18.6	56.1	119.5	225.7
1970[a]	37.8	50.2	96.6	196.6	381.2
1980[b]	37.6	58.7	151.2	286.2	533.7
1990[b]	32.5	76.6	142.6	420.1	671.8
2000[b]	28.7	94.9	179.4	552.8	855.8
			Net Electricity[c]		
1960[a]	4.6	10.6	5.1	0.7	21.0
1970[a]	14.8	15.8	16.2	0.2	47.0
1980[b]	28.8	26.4	27.7	0	82.9
1990[b]	54.3	46.2	36.2	0	136.7
2000[b]	81.5	66.3	44.3	0	192.1
			Total Including Electricity[d]		
1960[a]	47.6	55.7	73.8	121.8	298.9
1970[a]	88.4	104.5	152.2	197.1	542.2
1980[b]	137.0	149.9	246.9	286.2	820.0
1990[b]	219.9	236.0	330.7	420.1	1,206.7
2000[b]	309.8	323.6	437.0	552.8	1,623.2
			(Percent)		
			Total Excluding Electricity		
1960–70	1.8	10.6	5.6	5.1	5.4
1970–80	−0.1	1.6	4.6	3.8	3.4
1980–90	−1.3	2.7	−0.6	3.9	2.3
1990–2000	−1.1	2.2	2.3	2.6	2.5
			Net Electricity		
1960–70	12.3	4.1	12.1	—	8.4
1970–80	6.9	5.3	5.6	—	5.8
1980–90	6.6	5.7	2.7	0	5.1
			Total Including Electricity and Losses		
1960–70	6.4	6.5	7.5	4.9	6.1
1970–80	4.5	3.7	5.0	3.8	4.2
1980–90	4.8	4.6	3.0	3.9	3.9
1990–2000	3.5	3.2	2.8	2.6	3.0

[a]Actual.
[b]Forecast.
[c]Consumed by end-users.
[d]Includes losses in generation and transmission.
Source: Division of Economic and Business Research, University of Arizona, July 1981.

enacted. The public would react to these periods of strain by reducing its consumption of petroleum, using ride sharing, mass transit, improved scheduling of trips, and so forth. Marginal adjustments in ordinary ways of doing business would occur, but no drastic, permanent changes in lifestyles would be required.

The higher prices and greater supply uncertainties for conventional fuels would stimulate more rapid development of synthetics, renewable resources, and new end-use technologies that could reduce the dependence on vulnerable fuel supplies; however, renewable resources would not exceed one-fifth of total supplies nationally. Government would provide greater support for new energy development and conservation, but the stimulus would come chiefly from the private sector, through the price system.

Case C. Low Energy Use—Serious Extended Supply Problems.

This case assumes that energy constraints, brought on by international conditions, would be more severe and prolonged than in Case B. Foreign oil supplies might not be available for extended periods in the volumes demanded by the U.S. market, since overseas producers may restrict exports or the U.S. government might feel compelled to limit imports. Alternatively, it might levy a heavy tariff on them and thus open a wide gap between domestic and world prices. Energy prices would be very high. Federal policies would emphasize reductions in energy demand as well as alternative supply development. Energy efficiency standards might be imposed on a wide range of energy-using structures and appliances, as well as on vehicles. The nation's economy might be seriously dislocated at times, especially if the energy crises came in the form of sudden shocks rather than gradually over a period of years. U.S. energy consumption would fall another 25 percent from the level of Case B to 44 percent below Case A.

In Arizona, per capita energy consumption would also fall sharply, and total consumption in 2000 would be only slightly above the current level. The very high energy prices and supply uncertainties would induce residents to institute fairly drastic conservation measures, for example, buying smaller homes, many of them attached; moving closer to places of work; and cutting optional driving to a minimum. Mandatory measures, such as installation of prescribed insulation and prohibition of non-essential fuel uses, might be enacted on the state level. These measures would encroach on preferred lifestyles and would be viewed as standard of living reductions by many, although others might view them as an improvement.

Strong encouragement to develop America's renewable resources would accompany these changes, especially greater use
of solar and perhaps geothermal and biomass energy. The market for these sources would be limited, however, because of the
shrinkage in total energy consumption. We assume no serious
problems with nuclear power and coal-based electricity, so the
scarcity would be largely confined to liquid fuels.

Comparison of Three Scenarios

The Case A forecast was developed by means of a series of
regression equations representing the relationships between
energy consumption and various socioeconomic factors in-
fluencing it. Cases B and C were determined by applying the
implied percentage reductions in average U.S. energy consumption per capita from the Case A level to the Arizona projections.

The results for all three cases are shown in Table 3.3 and
Figure 3.1. As expected, the results for the three cases vary
widely. In Case A, Arizona's total energy consumption nearly
doubles over the twenty-year period, while in Case C the increase is very modest (11 percent). On a per capita basis, consumption increases moderately in Case A but falls in both of the
other cases—sharply in Case C. This reduction reflects lower
energy use by all sectors of the state's economy, not merely consumption in the residential and transportation sectors.

Table 3.3   *Arizona Annual Energy Consumption Under*
Three Assumptions
(Trillion Btus)

	Case A	Case B	Case C
1980	820.0	820.0	820.0
1990	1,206.7	1,121.6	1,005.8
2000	1,623.2	1,217.4	912.8
Annual Energy Consumption per Capita (Million Btus)			
1980	306	306	306
1990	334	310	278
2000	335	266	200
Annual Rate of Change (percent)			
1980–90	3.9	3.2	2.1
1990–2000	3.0	0.8	−0.9

Source: Division of Economic and Business Research, University of Arizona.

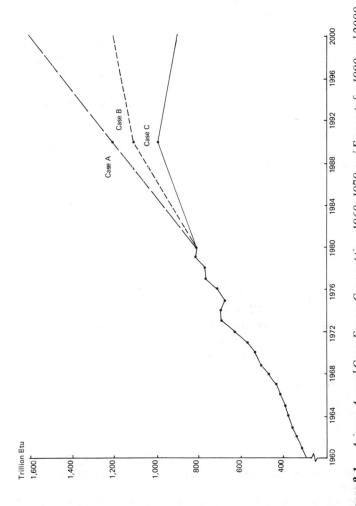

Figure 3.1   *Arizona Annual Gross Energy Consumption, 1960–1979 and Forecasts for 1990 and 2000*

Sources: Actual—U.S. Department of Energy, State Data Report.
Forecast—Division of Economic and Business Research, University of Arizona.

Some of the apparent inconsistencies the careful reader may detect, such as non-symmetrical results for the first and second decades of the forecast period, reflect the fact that neither the energy modeling techniques nor the socioeconomic or the energy forecasts are fully refined at this stage; considerably more work remains to be done before one can have complete confidence in such exercises.* In addition, the divergence between Case A and Case B reflects genuine uncertainty as to the growth of Arizona's energy demand in the face of unknown trends of future prices and supplies and consumer responses to them. Finally, it is impossible, at this time, to determine precisely the role of solar, geothermal, and other renewable resources in Arizona's energy future.

There is little doubt that the economy of Arizona and the lifestyles of its residents can accommodate themselves to a broad range of energy situations, provided that adequate lead time is available and that timely and effective measures are taken. The energy future is highly uncertain, and a repetition of the sudden shocks we have experienced twice already—possibly in more severe form—is more likely to occur than not. The current world oil surplus and OPEC's temporary inability to raise prices should not obscure this basic reality. Rather, responsible decision makers and the general public would do well to look beyond the current lull and prepare for future contingencies.

Arizona's Electric Power Balances

As of January 1, 1981, the capacity of electric power plants located in Arizona, plus the capacity owned by Arizona utilities located in other states, amounted to about 10,500 megawatts (Mw). Some 1,400 Mw of Arizona's capacity are owned by or committed to companies in California and Nevada, while about 9,100 Mw are available for supplying Arizona requirements (see Table 3.4).

Additional power plant construction underway or planned in Arizona through 1989 amounts to over 5,500 Mw. Of this total, some 3,700 Mw will be available to Arizona companies, and about 1,800 is owned by others. This includes 1,743 Mw (about 46 percent) of the Palo Verde Nuclear Project's total capacity of 3,810 Mw.

Ignoring short-term sales, Arizona has been a net importer of electricity but will become a net exporter in 1984, when Palo

---

*The failure of demand growth in Case A to slow down after 1990, even though the annual percentage increase is lower, is due to the higher starting base (in 1990 compared with 1980). In volume terms, annual increases actually become slightly larger.

Table 3.4 *Arizona Thermal Electric Generating Capacity, 1981–1989 (Megawatts)*

As of January 1, 1981	Arizona Owners	Other Owners	Total
Located in Arizona	6,841	1,408	8,247
Located Outside Arizona	2,242	4,154[a]	6,396
Total	9,083	5,562	14,645
(Net Imports = 2,242–1,408 = 834)			
Planned Additions, 1981–1989			
Located in Arizona	3,739	1,818	5,557
Total, December 31, 1989			
Located in Arizona	10,580	3,226	13,806
Located Outside Arizona	2,242	4,154[a]	6,396
Total	12,822	7,380	20,202
(Net Exports = 3,226–2,242 = 984)			

[a]Includes only plants in which Arizona companies have an interest.
Source: Western Systems Coordinating Council.

Verde Unit 2 is completed.* Arizona, however, will remain a net importer of energy overall as long as oil and gas retain a large share of the state's total energy mix, unless major reserves of these fuels are discovered within the state's borders. Arizona will continue to import large volumes of coal for several of its fossil fuel plants; in fact, as of 1982 there were no plans to operate any units other than the Navajo plant at Page on Arizona coal.

The decision by non-Arizona companies on where to locate generating capacity is a complex one. The restrictions placed by California laws and regulations on building power plants in that state—whether nuclear, coal, or other fossil fuel—have forced some California companies to look to locations outside the state as sites for additional generating capacity.

Electric power plants located in Arizona but built to generate power for export have been responsible for producing both costs and benefits for residents of the state. Among the costs are the use of Arizona's resources, including water, social costs, and environmental damages. Benefits include employment and

---

*Since the major Arizona electric utilities have considerable generating capacity in excess of local requirements, they have been in a position to export large volumes of power on a short-term basis. If these are included, the state has been a net electricity exporter since 1976.

income for Arizona residents and taxes paid to local governments; these are typically very large, since power plants are capital-intensive and property taxes reflect the value of plant and equipment.

An objective judgment on whether long-term electricity exports are beneficial to Arizona should be based on a comparison of all direct and indirect benefits accruing to the state and its residents and all costs for which such exports are responsible. If Arizona receives net benefits exceeding those it could obtain from using the same resources to produce alternative products, then it is worthwhile to devote resources to the export of electricity. This is the well-established principle of comparative advantage, according to which a nation or state will maximize the welfare of its citizens by exporting goods and services that it can produce relatively more cheaply than others, and importing those items for which others have a relative cost advantage. There is no real difference in the policy implications following from this principle, whether it is applied to copper, food, fibers, semiconductors, or electricity; nor does it matter whether the item requires quantities of a resource that is considered especially scarce, such as water. If buyers outside Arizona are willing to pay for the item a price that covers the cost of all resources embodied in it, then the decision to produce for export is sound.

It should be noted that not only has this principle been generally recognized as correct in concept, but also it has been widely applied for many years. It constitutes the basis of the European Common Market, under which trade barriers between members were removed and unprecedented prosperity ensued. And, of course, it has been the basis of the high standard of living of the U.S. population since our beginnings as a nation. It is incorporated in the interstate commerce clause of the Constitution, which prohibits the states from interfering with the free flow of commerce among them.

Quite apart from constitutional restraints, it would not be to Arizona's advantage to place restrictions on either exports or imports of energy, provided that pricing conforms to the full-cost standard. Any attempt to follow a policy of artificially based self-sufficiency in energy or other areas would raise the cost of living to Arizona residents and the cost of production to Arizona business. Measures to alter the free flow of commerce among the states can be justified in terms of economics only where conditions do not permit the law of comparative advantage to operate fairly, for example, where the price at which an item is sold does not fully cover the private and social cost of the resources used in its production.

Chapter 4

Interactions and Tradeoffs

The energy problem is particularly complex because it involves an interaction between many areas that have traditionally been treated as being independent of each other, but which are actually highly interdependent. Thus, energy choices must take into account changing resources, technology, economics, demographics, institutions, and values. Moreover, the strands that link each of these with the others are multidirectional. Changes in the resource base affect costs, but rising costs stimulate the search for alternative resources and better technologies for finding and producing them, at the same time that they reduce the demand for the resources found. Furthermore, established values and lifestyles are not rigid over time but tend to adapt themselves to changes in economic conditions, reflecting changing resources and technologies.

Economics

Economic forces are important influences affecting energy availability and requirements. On the supply side, a valid generalization is that the expected return on investment in energy must be competitive with returns available on alternative investments generally, allowing for differences in risk, both commercial and political. If an oil company anticipates better earnings from investing in overseas operations, coal, real estate, motels, or mail order firms than in oil and gas production, other things being equal, it will consider channeling at least a portion of its capital into such non-oil operations. If a change in the economic or regulatory climate reverses this relationship, one should expect to see oil companies step up the acquisition of leases, hire more exploration crews, and increase the drilling of wells.

[35]

Furthermore, if prospective returns on oil and gas investments begin to look less favorable because the most promising
locations have been fully explored, it would be natural for oil
companies to show a greater interest in acquiring coal, uranium,
and oil shale leases, and perhaps even to begin turning in the
direction of such (to them) unaccustomed sources as solar
energy. On the other hand, if the high costs of building facilities
to process shale, converting coal into liquids or gases, or moving
gas from Alaska to the lower forty-eight states raise questions
concerning the profitability of the huge investments required,
private companies would probably not make the investment in
the absence of government subsidies.*

All this is as it should be in a competitive market economy,
where the prices consumers are willing to pay represent the
value of the incremental unit produced. This is how an efficient
allocation of resources is achieved, and social welfare maximized
(assuming all costs are considered).

Some have argued that for several reasons this competitive
model does not apply to energy. Domestic energy resources
may be controlled by a few very large firms with the power to
charge monopoly prices. World oil prices, it is argued, may be
set at noncompetitive levels by the operation of OPEC, an international cartel, and energy may be considered so essential for
many users that they feel they must buy it regardless of how high
prices are allowed to rise.

Each of these arguments has some validity, but none has as
much as its proponents suggest. Concentration in oil production, refining, and marketing is among the lowest of major U.S.
industries.[1] Although there are examples of interlocking direc-
torships, there is competition in many uses between oil, gas, and
electricity. Oil company earnings, except during periods of acute
crisis, have been comparable to earnings of industry generally.[2]
Oil company acquisition of coal and shale oil reserves may speed,
rather than retard, their development, since such acquisition
brings massive infusions of capital, technological skills, and
managerial acumen to weak or infant industries. Some oil companies would perhaps like to exercise control over retail prices,
especially gasoline, but numerous investigations have turned up
little evidence that they have been able to do so—if only because
of the watchful eyes of antitrust authorities.

---

*In the case of R+D which has no chance of paying off for very long periods
but which promises large returns to society—for example, nuclear fusion—
government support can be justified. This does not apply to cases where the
technology is known but economic conditions are not yet favorable, e.g., shale
oil or coal gasification.

The case of OPEC appears to be more damaging. During the 1970s, world oil prices rose from under $3 a barrel to an average of $35 a barrel (in constant 1981 dollars this is an increase from $14.40 to $35 a barrel), with most of the increases coming in two gigantic jumps. Members of the organization control some 60 percent of non-Communist oil production and an even greater share (77 percent) of proved reserves. They meet at least twice a year to determine a common pricing policy for all members.

Again, however, this is not the whole story. The 1973–74 price increases occurred at the end of an unprecedented boom in world oil demand which strained available supplies. Furthermore, ownership of Middle East oil shifted from private companies to the host governments. Since governments presumably are more secure in their titles to oil reserves, they tend to have longer planning horizons and lower discount rates.[3] The current price that is optimal for them would therefore be substantially higher than the price for private owners. The 1979 increases were led by the "spot" market, which is highly competitive, and were caused by frantic efforts on the part of buyers to stock up on supplies because of the revolution in Iran. OPEC merely followed the market up.

Subsequent events have shown that OPEC is far from immune to the pressures of market forces. The second major price increase accelerated forces that were set in motion by the first increase: expanded oil production from non-OPEC sources (Mexico, Alaska, the North Sea), shifts from oil to coal and nuclear, and much greater fuel consumption efficiency. In addition, the macroeconomic impact of major oil price increases (higher inflation and worsening payment deficits) contributed to a general economic slowdown in Europe and North America. The result has been a virtually zero increase in overall energy consumption, actual reductions in world oil demand, and even greater cuts in the demand for OPEC oil (from about 31 million barrels per day in 1977 to less than 21 million barrels per day in October 1981).[4] Thus, even though Iran and Iraq, two major Middle East producers, were still at war as of late 1981 and produced only a fraction of their normal volumes, a sizeable surplus of oil has existed for some time. In part, this has been the consequence of a deliberate effort by Saudi Arabia to force the high-price OPEC producers to lower their prices. But it points out the fact that OPEC has never possessed the full regalia of a true cartel, with power to allocate production quotas when prices weaken. The interests of its thirteen members are too diverse to permit agreement on a durable price-output policy.

The "essentiality" argument, which implies that energy consumption is unresponsive to changes in energy prices, was widely accepted until quite recently. Energy demand was believed to march inexorably upward with time, population, and income, in a sort of "iron law of energy." Even the leading research institutions—and of course energy companies and government agencies—would project energy demand as a fixed ratio to economic growth. Other factors, including the fact that falling real energy prices boosted energy demand, received little or no attention.

Recent developments have produced ample evidence that this view is only limitedly correct. In the United States, energy consumption between 1973 and 1980 increased at the rate of 0.3 percent per year while the economy grew at an average rate of 2 percent per year (i.e., the energy-to-growth (E/G) ratio was a mere 0.15). By contrast, during 1960–73, energy consumption and economic growth both had moved at an average 4.1 percent per year (implying an E/G ratio of 1.0).[5] U.S. demand for petroleum products peaked in 1978 at 18.8 million barrels per day (MBD) and has fallen some 2.8 million barrels per day since then. This has permitted oil imports to the United States to be reduced from 8.5 MBD in 1977 to 5.5 MBD in 1981, or 35 percent. If this trend continues, the country will achieve substantial energy self-sufficiency before the end of the century even if domestic supplies of liquids cannot be increased.[6]

Conservation

Conservation must be a supporting foundation in any energy future. Essentially, the question is not of an either/or nature, i.e., do you favor conservation or the development of new energy technologies? Rather, conservation is a necessary complement to existing and developing technologies and supply options. Conservation is a barrel of oil not consumed, and therefore not produced. For every unit of energy saved or displaced by a given measure of technology, resources are saved, and the annual maintenance costs of producing energy are eliminated. For example, in several climate zones, $5 worth of Fiberglas insulation will buy a $35 barrel of oil (in energy equivalence terms). In this respect, conservation is frequently "the least cost energy strategy" in many uses and locations.[7]

The term *conservation* by energy users* refers to reductions in energy consumption, both price-induced ones and others. In

---

*Conservation in producing an exhaustible resource refers to an optimal production pattern over time.

principle, and for policy purposes, it is appropriate to differ-
entiate between the two types, although in practice it is difficult
to separate them. The first type, price-induced reductions in
energy usage, should refer to a shift in resource allocation, for
both consumers and energy-using firms, from that which had
existed during the period of low energy prices—for example,
substituting insulation for some gas heating and electric cooling.
Price-induced conservation is the principal reason why domestic
oil refineries are now operating at less than 70 percent of capacity and producing petroleum products 24 percent more effi-
ciently than in 1973, and why major oil companies are closing
thousands of service stations and withdrawing from long-
established market positions, and it is at least a major factor in
the widespread postponement and cancellation of electric power
plant construction. The price elasticities (the percentage reduction in demand due to a given percentage increase in price) of
energy demand in the short run, when consumers are con-
strained by existing appliances and cars, may be quite low, often
in the range of 0.1 to 0.2. Evidence is accumulating, however,
that if consumers are given time to adjust their stocks of
appliances and automobiles, they will opt for more efficient
ones, so long-run price elasticities tend to be much higher, often
above 1.0.[8] Price-induced energy conservation, the pocketbook
response of energy users, thus turns out to be a major factor in
any solution of the energy problem, although efforts to increase
both conventional and alternative supplies are also essential.

The second type of energy conservation represents changes
in tastes for consumers (towards less energy-intensive goods
and services) and changes in technology for producers (toward
energy-saving equipment). It is important to emphasize that
such changes need not seriously damage the socioeconomic or
life-quality amenities Americans have come to expect. Indeed,
a study of the energy requirements of expected lifestyles,
conducted by the Stanford Research Institute for the State of
California, concluded that conservation will be vital to lifestyle
maintenance.[9] Furthermore, a report by the U.S. General Accounting Office points out that an "aggressive conservation and
renewable resource program" in Arizona, California, and
Nevada could reduce electrical needs in the region by nearly 20
percent by the year 2000. The GAO adds that if the amount of
capital needed for new plant construction were shifted to such a
program it would offer great benefits "from the standpoint of
environment, equity, economy, and risk." Moreover, it "would
demand little change in lifestyle for the general public."[10]

Residential and commercial buildings are prime candidates
for energy conservation activities. Since buildings are replaced

very slowly and more than two-thirds of the existing stock of residential housing is below energy efficient standards, retrofitting is essential if residential and commercial energy usage is to become more efficient any time soon.[11] Research has indicated that cost has been the most common barrier to retrofitting.[12] However, the knowledge of what can and ought to be done to improve the energy efficiency of a building is a prerequisite to any form of energy conservation, be it retrofitting or new construction. When a building owner either does not know what can be done for the building, or knows what can be done but does not know what would be cost-effective, then lack of knowledge becomes the first barrier to energy conservation.[13]

In industry, where cost considerations typically are paramount, direct fuel savings of up to 30–40 percent have already been achieved by efficiency measures and energy-saving devices.[14] Improvements in heat-transfer efficiencies and management of waste heat are bringing additional savings to industry. Considerable research is also underway to develop new energy-efficient equipment and processes. Indirect savings are also being explored. For example, in the agricultural sector in Arizona, where pumping costs are high, considerable attention is being given to the development of more energy-efficient ways to use irrigation water.

In a rapidly growing state like Arizona, where population is expected to double in twenty years (3.5 percent annual growth rate), energy-efficient new construction in all sectors of the economy will play an important role. Arizona has established state building code guidelines for new construction. These codes provide specific guidelines for local governments for energy-efficient new construction in all areas of the state.[15] Work on codes is also progressing in the solar energy area.[16] These state guidelines are strictly optional; only local codes can be enforced.

Yet, any time new methods or procedures are put into operation, there are time and financial costs. Time is required to become accustomed to new regulations, for materials to be delivered, for engineers to redesign building plans, and for the labor force to learn new work patterns. Personnel involved in each step must be paid for their time, thus making the initial implementation of the new energy regulations costly. Tradeoffs in new and efficient construction, therefore, must be evaluated over the long run. Length of payback periods becomes a crucial point in gaining acceptance of the new construction techniques, especially during times of high interest rates. However, results have shown that the payback for most construction techniques required by energy regulations often is quite moderate. For example (using the Arizona guidelines), when construction techniques were modified to increase insulation, through energy-efficient doors and windows and properly installed caulking and sealing, the price of a single family dwelling increased, but the payback in energy savings was figured to be less than four years.

Such evidence as exists indicates that the bulk of total conservation to date can be explained purely as a response to higher energy prices, i.e., it represents movement in the direction of efficient energy use. The complete range of conservation options has by no means been fully used. People are not sufficiently informed about the energy-saving actions they can take. A 1978 survey conducted in Arizona showed that consumers are vitally interested in saving energy, but feel they do not have enough information about which energy-saving measures are effective and economically sound.[17] Most Arizona residents have no real idea which measures work and are cost-effective, where to begin and how to budget, or what degree of technical competence is required for various projects. Many homeowners easily recognize the value of insulation or solar devices, but overlook less costly but effective activities including draft control and window treatments.[18] It therefore seems apparent that if energy conservation programs are to be fully developed and implemented, then a deeper understanding of consumer behavior and decision-making patterns must be obtained. What is needed is an understanding of the role that individual values, standards, and goals play in energy decision-making and, beyond that, in energy-related quality of life changes (both positive and negative).

Additional evidence that Arizona residents are interested in conservation and solar are shown in tax returns filed for Arizona tax credits (Table 4.1); the figures represent a minimum, since not all installations are listed in tax returns. Both the number of

Table 4.1   *Arizona Solar and Conservation Tax Credits**

Year	Number of Tax Returns	Total Dollar Value	Average Tax Return
1978	2,839	$ 949,468	$334
1979	9,316	5,034,633	540
1980**	13,314	7,927,621	595

*Combined returns and dollar values of solar and conservation tax credits taken for Arizona.
**Through July 14, 1981 (approximately 70% complete).
Source: Arizona Department of Revenue.

returns and the dollar value per return have been rising, indicating an increasing impact on future energy use.

Environmental Constraints and Risks

No energy source is environmentally completely benign; each has its own environmental costs and attendant risks. Environmental risks occur both in the work environment and more generally, in the form of concern or anxiety about the environment. All energy sources can have adverse effects on air or water quality, damage the land, injure human health or safety, and have negative socioeconomic effects, although the severity ranges widely from place to place and among sources.

Numerous environmental regulations, particularly those relating to air pollution, acid mine drainage, and surface mining and reclamation, have been enacted in the past several years to protect citizens from the environmentally damaging side effects of energy production. Some political and industrial leaders have argued that many of these environmental laws are excessive and impose unreasonable burdens on the energy industry and the national economy. They advocate rescinding or modifying many current statutes and regulations, claiming that such actions would help alleviate potential energy shortfalls. While there is broad agreement about the need to readdress costs and other specific aspects of environmental regulation, it is not obvious that environmental constraints are the primary obstacle to future energy production. Escalating costs, high interest rates, disappointing geological prospects, and limited water availability in the West are other significant constraining elements.

Failure now to adequately protect land, air, and water resources may in the long run create problems that will be far more costly to correct. For example, the problem with the most serious potential consequences is the climatic impact of continued increase in the upper atmosphere of carbon dioxide from fossil fuel combustion.[19] Some of these impacts will be irreversible. Many of the most intractable environmental problems we face today are a result of past failures to recognize or cope with the externalities associated with certain energy developments; that is, energy supplies, air, and water were considered and used as free resources, and the expenses of cleaning up those resources were not incorporated into their operating costs. Unless these extended costs are accounted for in the price mechanism, what may appear as an attractive and viable short-term solution may, in the long run, be quite counterproductive when all associated risks and external costs are evaluated.

Arizona citizens are clearly concerned about the adverse environmental impacts of energy development. Within the western states, with significant amounts of domestic energy reserves, there are examples of boomtown development, strip mining, air and water quality changes, and productive land converted to energy production. Citizens are supportive of energy development in general, but when the local environmental costs become too high they tend to have second thoughts.[20]

While there are environmental and social risks associated with any future energy source development, there are also risks in doing nothing or in overcommitting to only one option. For example, if a Three Mile Island situation occurred a second or third time, it is almost certain there would be significant public pressures to reevaluate and possibly phase out nuclear energy. If such a thing did occur, however, and we were heavily dependent upon that single source of energy, the problem of potential energy shortages would be magnified. In the absence of other environmentally and economically acceptable technologies to take up the slack, there might be no viable alternative except to continue with the technology, i.e., to learn to live with its risks and costs while other alternatives were being explored. Overcommitment to any single technology, or even conservation alternative, entails risk, and range of alternatives is thus desirable. Since energy is required for the development of new energy resources, the best time to develop new sources is when current sources are not in short supply.

Waste

An important environmental and land-use issue is what to do with the residuals left by energy production activities. The disposal of coal slag is a problem that dates back to the early 19th century and is still not fully resolved. Otherwise promising new sources, such as geothermal, also raise environmental questions involving waste disposal. Liquid wastes from geothermal systems can be highly saline or toxic, and must either be injected back into the ground or evaporated in impermeable ponds.

The storage and disposal of nuclear waste, however, are perhaps the most controversial waste-related issues confronting the public today. Storage of nuclear wastes implies the possibility that they may be recovered at some future date if a superior storage or disposal system is developed or if an original miscalculation proves to have been made, or if a unique technological use for some of the stored isotopes should develop. Disposal implies the permanent placement of the wastes without either the possibility or intent of retrieving them.

In Arizona the nuclear-waste issue arises because while other states derive power from nuclear facilities located in Arizona, there is no evidence that they will take a proportional share of the resulting wastes. It is entirely possible that all nuclear wastes ultimately will be deposited in federally operated repositories located out of state. In this event, the waste disposal problem for Arizona becomes one of transportation (except for temporary storage at the power plant), with the related issues of safety and security from vandalism and terrorism.

If, however, no state is willing or can be forced to be a repository for wastes from other states, each state may be required to solve its own nuclear waste disposal problems. (A 1980 court case, overturning a Washington State ballot proposition prohibiting out-of-state wastes from entering the state, may lead to further litigation to settle the question.) Arizona may yet be selected as a national repository. While the state had not been selected for early testing and development as of 1981, southern Arizona has been designated for study as a potential site for high-level waste disposal.

Whether stored or disposed of, high-level radioactive nuclides must be kept from accidental contact with the atmosphere, biosphere, and hydrosphere for very long periods.* The length of time that nuclear wastes must be stored in isolation might be judged by looking at the time required for the waste to decay to the level of radioactivity of a normal uranium ore body. For high-level wastes, this is less than 10,000 years. For spent fuel (no reprocessing) the period is less than 100,000 years.

If high-level radioactive wastes are disposed of by currently suggested methods and if nuclear fuel reprocessing is permitted, the Palo Verde Nuclear Generating Station (given a forty-year operating life) will require about forty acres of underground storage space. This area can be reduced if a delay between reprocessing and burial is allowed. If nuclear fuel reprocessing is not practiced, the spent fuel and the fuel assemblies must be sequestered. This would increase the space requirement over twenty-five times.

The steps involved in high-level radioactive waste storage and disposal are interim storage as a liquid, conversion to a solid, transportation, and storage or disposal in a surface or subsurface repository. Among the methods proposed are the following: (1) deposition in bedded salt and salt domes. This is the method most studied, and it is considered the most suitable for disposal; however, the disposal is usually considered ultimate, with little or no chance of retrieval; (2) deposition in thick shale or clay sequences; (3) reposition in tunnels, or dry mines in

---

*During its estimated forty-year life, the Palo Verde plant will also produce 17.2 million cubic feet of low-level radioactive waste, which must also be disposed of.

granite or desert hills; (4) deposition in unsaturated zones in desert environments; (5) the construction of pyramids in a desert environment; and (6) nuclear transmutation of the long-lived nuclides to short-lived species, a process that reduces the necessary containment period. All of these methods, and others, have received at least some continuing study, as have several methods of waste solidification. As yet, however, agreement has not been reached on a national approach to be adopted.

Among the host rocks considered, the level of scientific knowledge is greatest for salt, followed by granite, basalt, and tuff, respectively. Investigations of other potential host rocks, including unsaturated rocks and shale, are being conducted, but at a lower level of effort.

In the state of Arizona, bedded salt deposits of 10,000 or more feet in thickness lie in an area west of Phoenix and northeast of Kingman (the Red Lake and Luke Basins). Thick shale or clay sequences of 100–6000 meters exist in the plateau portion of the state. Unsaturated desert zones can be found in such areas as Black Mesa and the Coconino plateau. It is also possible that acceptable non-fractured granite may be found at depths below 3000 feet in northern Arizona. Finally, shallower, more accessible granite formations exist in the southern portion of the state, but they may be too fractured. While there does not appear to be a lack of candidate locations for storage and disposal in Arizona, and while only one may be needed, considerably more geological and hydrogeologic mapping and testing will be required in order to gather sufficient evidence to make an intelligent choice.

Perceptions among both the scientific community and the public about the risks associated with nuclear-waste handling vary widely. Some contend that nuclear wastes can be stored in properly chosen underground repositories with no hazard to the public, while others maintain that these wastes cannot easily be so stored and represent irreversible health and environmental hazards.[21]

Since a high-level-waste underground disposal facility has yet to be built, any cost estimates are speculative. While mining costs might be used as the starting point or basis for estimation, these are likely to be inadequate and prove to be too low. A principal consideration is the engineering required to maintain the very long-term integrity of the surrounding material and containers.

Table 4.2 presents a very rough estimate of the facility costs for the construction, operation, and closure of a high-level radioactive waste disposal site. The numbers presented should, however, be subject to a large margin of error. Presumably the cost uncertainty would be narrowed after a specified site has

Table 4.2   *High-Level Radioactive Waste Disposal Facility Costs*
             (1980)

Rock Type	Cost per Metric Ton of Spent Fuel	Total Facility Costs
Salt	$52,000	$4,607,000
Granite	78,000	6,911,000
Shale	57,000	5,050,000
Basalt	87,000	7,708,000

Sources: U.S. DOE, *Final Environmental Impact Statement: Management of Commercially Generated Radioactive Waste,* DOE/EIS-0046F, Vol. 1, October, 1980; Interagency Review Group on Nuclear Waste Management, *Report to the President,* TID-29442, March, 1979. (Assumes 148 GW_e nuclear capacity in 2000 and accumulated waste through 2005.)

been chosen. The selection process itself will serve to identify the particular rock structures, their hardness, the type of overburden and other geomechanical and mining factors. Additional cost uncertainties will diminish as facility operating, construction, and waste packaging technologies are further developed.

Assuming the total facility costs for a salt based depository shown in Table 4.2, the share based on Palo Verde's output of electricity would be roughly $118 million in 1980 dollars. Inflation will undoubtedly increase this. However, as a proportion of the estimated cost of the Palo Verde facility, even if the costs are 50 percent higher on a current basis, the effect will not be great when averaged across all of the utility's power generating costs at all plants and across the consumer rate structure. Disposal costs in fact represent only a small part of the total cost of electricity.

Finally, it should be noted that the estimate is based on multi-user disposal facilities. If Arizona must store its own wastes, the economies of scale available in mining and engineering of containers and structures would be lost, and unit costs could be two to four times as great. This loss results from the geometry of the structures, the commonality of some of the structures regardless of facility size, the commonality of site exploration and development costs regardless of size, and the difference in borrowing and discount rates between companies and the federal government. Even if amortized over a long period, the effects on electric rates would be noticeable. In addition, there will be substantial decommissioning costs for the Palo Verde plant.

It should be noted that, if and when spent, fuel processing and waste management procedures have been demonstrated to be acceptable from the technical, the environmental, and the societal viewpoints; a "nuclear park" on a state preserve providing fuel fabrication and processing facilities for all of the nuclear power generating stations in the Southwest would give Arizona a major new industrial asset.

Water Issues

One of the major resource constraints within Arizona is the availability of fresh or low-salinity water. The production of almost any future energy source within Arizona will make additional claims on the state's water supplies. There is no general agreement on whether there is adequate water available to meet projected energy demands; the answer depends on the analyst's specific assumptions. What is clear, however, is that reallocation among consuming sectors will have to occur if large amounts of water are used for energy production, and also that water quality will change if large-scale energy development is undertaken in Arizona.

Water demand for energy production is coming at a time when other users are claiming more. Rapidly growing cities such as Phoenix and Tucson, as well as many smaller communities, are planning for continued growth and are moving to insure an adequate supply of water for future as well as current residents. Arizona's Indian tribes are also demanding their fair share, but it is not yet clear how much water this will entail or how the solution of the Indian water rights question will affect other users. To examine the water requirements for energy without considering the needs and demands of other claimants would be to lose sight of the interdependencies of water and energy in Arizona's future, as well as the profound social and economic implications that water reallocation to energy will have.

Arizona would not face a serious water problem were it not for the dwindling supply of fresh water and the remote likelihood of augmenting it.[22] The only large source of surface water is the Colorado River and its tributaries, including the Salt River. How much water actually flows in the Colorado is a matter of some public controversy. The negotiators of the Colorado River Compact of 1922 allocated 7.5 million acre feet each to the upper and lower basins but assumed an average annual flow of just under 17 million acre feet. The actual measured virgin flow of the Colorado River, during what hydrologists identify as a dry cycle, from 1931–1968, averaged 13.2 million acre feet. The Bureau of Reclamation's long-term estimate (based on the period from 1896) is 14.9 million acre feet. Researchers using dendrochronology techniques to estimate still longer periods have come up with a substantially lower figure of 13.5 million acre feet.[23] Whatever the precise amount that may in fact be available, it is certain that formal allocations to the various states in the Colorado River basin and to Mexico have exceeded what is physically available. The reason the overcommitment is not yet painfully obvious is that the Upper Basin states have not yet developed their total allocations.

Water consumption for energy will also mean greater salinity in an already saline Colorado River. This could decrease the usefulness of its waters for some purposes. It could also result in increased policy conflict with Mexico over the quality of water delivered to its citizens.

Groundwater is the other major source of water in Arizona. Over thousands of years, the earth has stored substantial amounts of water beneath the arid landscape. However, in some places irrigated agriculture and municipal users have "mined" the aquifers, withdrawing water at rates far faster than the slow recharging process. Groundwater tables have been falling precipitously in some areas, including Tucson, the largest metropolitan area in the nation that is entirely dependent on groundwater.

In 1980 the Arizona legislature passed the Groundwater Management Act, the goal of which is to balance groundwater withdrawal and the rate of replenishment (generally by the year 2025). The act established four Active Management Areas (AMAs). Any new industrial user of groundwater in an AMA who does not have a grandfather right, or who wants to expand his use beyond what his grandfather right entitles him to, can attempt to either purchase an existing grandfather right which can be converted to his use, obtain a permit to pump from the Department of Water Resources, or obtain service from a city or private water company (if available). New industrial permits will be issued only after the intended use satisfactorily meets a number of criteria, including that of showing adequate supply for the intended life of the project and the non-availability of sewage effluent or CAP water. These provisions of the act will encourage the recycling of water and increased competition for effluent. Energy supply projects planned for the four AMAs will be subject to the act's restrictions.

If the goal of the act is met, increases in pumping costs should slow, since pumpers will not be increasing their energy costs by digging deeper to reach water. The first management plans for each AMA, which will include water conservation requirements for all classes of users, are due in January 1983. Statewide, new wells with a discharge over 35 gallons per minute must be registered and must comply with well-construction standards. In addition, wells in AMAs and in areas designated as irrigation non-expansion areas must be measured and an annual report made of water use.

Stretching available supplies through storage and diversion, once made possible by federal subsidies to construction, no longer appears to be a feasible strategy. Most dam sites have already been used, reservoirs have environmental and social impacts, and areas of origin for diversions object to the loss of water. Furthermore, the Office of Management and Budget regularly exercises its budget scissors on proposals for new Western water projects. The Carter Administration articulated a new approach to water policy that emphasized conservation and water management rather than increased water supply. Administration officials dramatically displayed their commitment to end large-scale federally subsidized water development programs by reevaluating a number of water resource projects for possible deauthorization, including the Central Arizona Project (CAP). While the Reagan Administration supports the construction of the CAP, additional projects that would substantially relieve the emphasis on water development are less likely than they once were.

Water issues are particularly acute with regard to energy produced within Arizona for export to other states, primarily California. The question is one of allocating water supplies for producing energy which will not be used in Arizona, although the exports generate income for Arizona residents. The point is that if water that is in limited supply is used for electrical power generation for export it must come at the expense of agricultural land taken out of production, or of municipal or industrial development foregone in Arizona. (This relationship should be viewed symmetrically: land developed for agriculture is at the expense of electric development.) Different alternative energy sources imply different amounts of water exported. For example, a nuclear power plant uses more water than a similar-sized coal-fired power plant. Of the power produced by Palo Verde, 53.4 percent will be exported, implying a net water export of 14,420 acre feet per year above the amount that a coal-fired plant would have required. The water export question, however, is not unique to the tradeoffs between water and energy. Similar questions have been raised in the past relative to agricultural produce being grown with Arizona water and shipped out of the state.

Transportation and Land Use

Arizona used up over 1.4 billion gallons of motor fuel (538 gallons per capita) per year as of 1981, some 19 percent above the national average. Nearly two-thirds of the state's total petroleum use went for transportation, against 53 percent for the nation. Because of Arizona's high usage in the transportation sector, and the transportation sector's high dependency on oil, Arizona is quite vulnerable to disruptions in oil supply.

Transportation in Arizona consists predominantly of passenger transportation (see Figure 4.1). Statewide, in 1975 only about one-sixth of transportation energy went for freight movement by truck. Railroads used only 2.4 percent of energy, while pipelines used 8 percent. Over two-thirds of the transportation-energy was used to move people. And, since only 8 percent of the total was used for airline transportation, while buses took 0.3 percent, the bulk was for passenger vehicles plus pickups. Indeed, these vehicles accounted for nearly 64 percent of the transportation energy in Arizona. In addition, it was found that twice as many of the vehicle-miles traveled in the state were for shopping or pleasure than were for trips to work.[24]

A study of the Phoenix metropolitan area indicated a 70-percent reduction in urban transportation-energy consumption could be achieved by the year 2000 through changes in the operation and use of transportation systems.[25] The three changes with the greatest potential are: (1) increases in fuel economy of automobiles; (2) increases in occupancy rates of automobiles; and (3) reductions in discretionary automobile trips. An increase in auto fuel economy from an average of 11.9 mpg to 30.3 mpg would, by itself, reduce total fuel consumption in the year 2000 by about 50 percent.

By contrast, other transportation system changes would produce only modest reductions in energy consumption. A ninefold increase in public transit usages, for example, would reduce consumption by only 1 percent because base transit ridership is so low (only 0.5 percent of total trips in the Phoenix metropolitan area) and transit load factors are so low (13 percent occupancy).[26] Arizona's major cities are and will probably remain too dispersed to sustain transit systems appreciably larger than current ones, at least for some time to come. Primary attention is therefore more properly focused on the fuel economy of automobiles and the efficiency with which automobiles are used. But some large employers are offering bus or van service from central pickup points, and more could do so effectively.

There is good evidence to suggest, however, that if land-use patterns were to be changed, energy requirements would go down sharply. A study of the Washington, D.C., metropolitan area, for example, concluded that additional transportation energy use between 1976 and 1992 could be cut in half by strictly controlling land use to avoid low-density, contiguous development.[27] Even a conservative estimate of the transportation energy savings achievable through land-use controls put

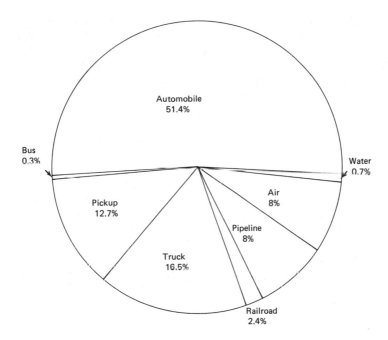

Figure 4.1 *Arizona Transportation Energy Consumption Patterns by Mode, 1975*

Source: Arizona Department of Transportation, Transportation Planning Division, *Arizona Transportation Energy: Usage Patterns,* December 1977.

them at about 15 percent.[28] Modification of land-use patterns could have a multiple effect on transportation. First, the number of trips could be reduced by locating some closely linked activities at the same site. Second, even where this is not possible, there is the potential for reducing the length of trips by putting the interacting activities closer together. Finally, the number of trips taken by the less efficient modes can be reduced through land-use changes. The potential is impressive, but the slowness of land-use changes—and the political resistance to some of them—is equally evident. Land-use patterns are not easily controlled by government and are not quick to change once in place. In Arizona, the historically low cost of land has led to highly dispersed and energy-inefficient patterns of land use. The Phoenix and Tucson metropolitan areas have population densities that rank them in the bottom 10 percent of all urbanized areas in the nation. The population densities of these urbanized areas actually declined in the decade of the 1970s.

To some extent, however, rising energy prices have already altered land-use patterns in Arizona's urban areas. For example, in both the Tucson and Phoenix metropolitan areas, development of certain neighborhoods on the urban fringe has followed the neighborhood unit idea to some extent. These neighborhoods are characterized by a core of single-family residential activity, surrounded by some multi-family, commercial, and in some cases light industrial land uses. This is one example of a mixed land-use pattern that economizes on transportation and energy requirements by allowing residents to locate near shopping and employment opportunities. Similar examples could be cited for other Arizona cities. A mixed land-use policy seeks an optimum blending of low- and high-intensity land uses. In contrast, traditional zoning fosters the spatial separation of uses traditionally considered incompatible. Since locating nonresidential activities close to residential areas generates both increased traffic noise and congestion, along with improved accessibility to employment and other activities, a policy of mixing land uses in urban areas should attempt to balance benefits and costs generated from the land use of urban land. Land uses can be mixed without depressing residential property values (an important component of which is the attractiveness of a residential area) if the quantity, quality, and spatial distribution of nonresidential activities are carefully thought out and adhered to.[29]

To implement an urban development policy of mixing land use, zoning changes would certainly be required, but state and local officials thus far show few signs of being prepared to depart drastically from current policy, and to embark upon such a range of mixed-use policies. Energy conservation is only one factor considered by producers and consumers when they make economic decisions on where to locate and how to use land, and other considerations are often of overriding concern to them. Yet should energy prices rise dramatically in real terms, and remain high long enough for people to accept the change as permanent, then residential densities might be expected to rise, albeit gradually, and mixing of land uses might be expected to increase.

The question of the amount of land required to generate and transport energy is another important transportation-land use question. Energy generation is itself an important land use, and sometimes a substantial amount of energy is required to transport fuel, notably coal, oil, and natural gas to the site of energy generation. Transportation is also required to clean up the after-effects and side-effects of energy generation. Potential energy sites, such as those associated with geothermal generation, need to be protected against the incursion of uses that would preclude their future use for this purpose. Such sites might be purchased outright through eminent domain, or, should this prove too costly, they might be protected by "energy easements." Regardless of the kind of energy involved, sites for energy generation and transmission must be viewed as the subject of statewide land policy.[30]

Institutional and Policy Considerations

Considerable expansion has occurred in state energy programs since the oil embargo of 1973–74. While there are several state agencies involved with energy activities, the three primary agencies are the Arizona Solar Energy Commission (ASEC), Arizona Energy Office (AEO), and the Arizona Corporation Commission. While each of these operates in a different institutional framework, there has been a close working relationship between the Arizona Solar Energy Commission and the Arizona Energy Office. The ASEC was established by the legislature in 1975 and the commissioners are appointed by the governor. The AEO was established within the Governor's Office of Economic Planning and Development in 1974. The AEO was initially an emergency fuel allocation operation because of the immediate problems resulting from the embargo; it has since developed into an overall energy office which addresses a number of energy information and conservation oriented activities. Certain programs, such as the Energy Extension Service, an energy outreach program, are divided between the ASEC and the AEO.

The ASEC has been significantly supported by the state over the years, with the federal government supplying less than one third of its operating budget ($379,600 of $1,166,900 total budget for 1981). Arizona has been a leader in developing major tax credits for solar energy, and the ASEC provides a number of grants for research and commercialization activities relating to solar in addition to educational programs.

The AEO initially did not have the same type of focus toward long-term solutions that was embodied in the goals of the ASEC, but rather was more involved with responding to day-to-day emergencies and administering some of the federally mandated laws relating to fuel allocation and conservation. In recent years the state legislature has significantly increased the operating budget of the AEO, but the federal government has continued to supply 80 to 90 percent of total funding ($2,624,600 of $2,798,400 total budget in 1981).

The Arizona Corporation Commission is constitutionally established, and exercises the powers of a public utilities or public service commission, as well as functions often guided by secretaries of state. As such, it has the power to set rate structures and specific rates for public utilities in the state. While the commission has long been involved in such rate proceedings, it has only been since the late 1970s, owing to the Public Utilities Regulatory Policies Act (PURPA) and changing energy prices, that the commission has begun to evaluate different approaches to rate making.

In addition to PURPA, a number of legislative programs, primarily federal, have resulted in new incentives and educational programs that encourage both energy conservation and solar energy development. Federal budget cutbacks, however, could jeopardize the existing Appropriate Technology Grants, the Solar Cities and Town Program, the Energy Extension Service, the Weatherization Assistance Program, Institutional Conservation and Emergency Planning, and the Solar and Conservation Bank. The current philosophy on these programs appears to be based on the view that decontrol of oil and gas prices will spur investments in conservation and renewable energy sources and that the government can now set aside and let market forces prevail.[31] Others, however, question the validity of this view, arguing that it overestimates market capabilities and that government involvement is needed to insure the market works to make the right shifts with sufficient speed.[32] A central question for Arizona is whether it should develop its own energy programs or whether with the removal of price controls, sufficient incentives now exist to prompt the private sector to move effectively towards solving the state's energy problems. If a state leadership role is appropriate, then the question becomes whether Arizona has the policy and administrative capabilities to manage these programs effectively.

Currently within Arizona, in the absence of any formal state policy, energy policy is established de facto by the major energy suppliers. Energy planning is based on data developed from the major energy suppliers, and there are no alternative long-term forecasts based on independent analysis and public debate of future possible energy supplies and requirements. Energy decisions are largely regional in nature (whether by government or by the private sector). Increasingly, sharing of information and energy modeling takes place at the regional level. Arizona, for example, participates in discussions with the Western Governors' Energy Policy Office, and in informal information exchanges with other Western states.

As changes occur during the 1980s, current incentives to energy suppliers and consumers, as well as the existing regulatory approach, may change to produce a vastly different institutional framework for Arizona energy issues. The many different questions involving decentralization versus centralization, energy supplying companies versus energy servicing companies, efficient energy use versus additional energy production, and independent data bases versus energy supplier data bases, will all be publicly debated because of the importance of the outcomes. Broad-based evaluation of energy options is not possible within the current activities of Arizona energy institutions.

Twice in recent years, in 1973–74 and again in 1979, the United States was hit by shortages of petroleum products brought about by events in the Middle East.[33] Given the concentration of world oil reserves in the Middle East and the fragility of peace and internal stability in that region, further interruptions in the flow of oil to world markets must be expected. As a 1980 report by the U.S. Senate put it, "Even if the present conflict between Iraq and Iran is settled quickly, a major oil supply disruption within the next decade is likely."[34] Future supply problems, however, will not take the same form and will not be handled in the same manner as previous ones. Both the earlier interruptions occurred at times when the U.S. oil industry was subject to price and allocation controls by federal agencies. Supplies were distributed by oil companies under a system of historical quotas approved by federal authorities. After priority uses (emergency services, agriculture, etc.) were filled, the general public had to obtain its supplies as best it could, by waiting in line at gas stations. The states, under a set-aside provision, were given the right to allocate a limited volume (5 percent of the total) to assist in the relief of hardship cases and emergency situations. A future supply problem is likely to take on a very different character, since federal policy under the Reagan Administration differs sharply from policies followed by the three previous presidents. According to the Office of Energy Contingency Planning, for any shortage but the most severe (in excess of 20 percent), market forces will be used to distribute available supplies. A 12 percent shortfall, such as that of 1973–74, is not considered severe enough to warrant federal intervention. This means that oil prices could at least double if the conditions of the first crisis repeat themselves.

In addition, the Emergency Petroleum Allocation Act, under which allocations to hard-hit areas were authorized, was allowed to expire in 1981, although a modified version of the act was passed in Congress in early 1982.[35] The President still has the authority to implement a national rationing program in the event of a major emergency, but planning of its details has not as yet been completed.

At the state level, a legislative attempt that was made to give the governor the power to do pre-crisis planning, and to allocate some gasoline as he did in the last shortage, failed. Thus the only powers the governor has are his general emergency powers. As of 1981, in the event of an actual shortage the governor would use his emergency powers, and anyone who objected could sue him after the fact. Legally, the Arizona Energy Office can provide only advice and technical assistance to localities. It does not have control over actual supplies and it cannot order oil companies to allocate to specific communities or end-uses. Without gubernatorial authority, the entire burden of coping with emergency conditions falls on local authorities. Few if any are prepared to discharge such responsibilities.

Recent political changes provide an opportunity to readdress the imbalance that once existed between state and federal roles in energy, as in other areas. Crucial opportunities could be lost if the policy and administrative requirements of Arizona's energy future are not considered at the same time and on the same scale as the specific technical requirements relating to either energy supply or conservation. As the federal government steps back from active energy decision-making and limits funding, the states need to reexamine their role in energy policy making. Arizona should consider the desirability of providing opportunities for public debate on various energy options, establishing an unbiased energy base, fostering educational opportunities, and encouraging local emergency planning. These activities would provide the state with the capability of addressing an uncertain energy future.

Part III

Selected Alternatives

Chapter 5

Solar Energy

Arizona stands out from other states for its abundance of solar energy and is also one of the leaders in the development and utilization of the solar resource. Over 30,000 solar systems were estimated to be in use in the state in 1981, mostly domestic hot water and pool heating systems, and the number of installations has been doubling nearly every year. Passive solar designs, active solar space heating (particularly in the cooler parts of the state), and a variety of commercial applications have been successfully sold and used. Solar cooling systems (of prime importance to Arizona's metropolitan centers), electricity production, irrigation pumping, and many other solar applications have been developed and demonstrated in the state.

Arizona passed one of the first solar tax incentive laws in 1974, and today ranks first in the nation with the most comprehensive package of tax incentives for both the residential and commercial use of solar energy, as well as for energy conservation. The residential tax credit of 35 percent, combined with the federal credit of 40 percent, provides a powerful incentive for solar use. The state's 35 percent commercial tax credit carries no upper limit. A variety of additional items of legislation addressing solar concerns has also been implemented; these include the licensing of solar contractors, warranty and standards requirements, regulations for local solar access planning, prohibition on new deed restrictions against solar use, and mandating of solar installations on new state buildings.

The Arizona Solar Energy Commission was established by the legislature in 1975 to encourage the development and use of solar energy and other renewable energy resources in the state. The Commission also provides solar information services, develops standards and codes, and administers a broad solar research and development program. There is also broad-based support for solar energy research and education in the state in both the public and private sectors.

Technology Status

Solar collectors are devices that convert the radiant energy from the sun directly into usable heat energy, or when photovoltaic (PV) cells are used, into electrical energy. Collectors can be active or passive, depending on whether external energy other than that from the sun must be supplied to the system. A properly designed house, for instance, can function as an integrated, passive collection system maintaining itself at a comfortable temperature throughout the year. On the other hand, the most widely used types of domestic solar water heaters rely on pumps, temperature sensors, relays, electronic controls, and often other components to sense the availability of solar energy, circulate water from a storage tank to the collectors and back, maintain the desired water temperature, and protect the system from freezing in cold weather. A properly designed system needs very little extra energy to do these tasks.

In either case, thermal collection is accomplished by allowing the sun to strike a dark surface that is in contrast with a working fluid, either gas or liquid, to which the absorbing surface can subsequently transfer its collected heat. This fluid is heated by the conduction of energy out of the collector material and into the fluid, where it is subsequently transported to its point of use as a heat source or for the production of electricity in generators. In the case of PV cells, the sunlight is converted directly to electricity in the cell itself and is available for use through a pair of wires connected to the cell array.

Owing to the relatively low density of solar energy (approximately 200 to 300 Btu/ft^2/hr), large areas of collectors are required to capture useful amounts of energy. This large-area requirement makes a solar energy system quite capital-intensive, and collector costs and performance become the dominant consideration. Moreover, in many cases storage of the collected energy is necessary to permit its use at times when no solar input is present.

Figure 5.1 shows how the annual total solar radiation (insolation) on the surface of the earth is distributed in the United States.[2] Each line connects all points with a common value. It can readily be seen that the areas with the greatest amounts are centered in the Southwest, with Arizona enjoying a major portion of the area of maximum solar energy input. This maximum, which is on the order of one kilowatt per square meter (317

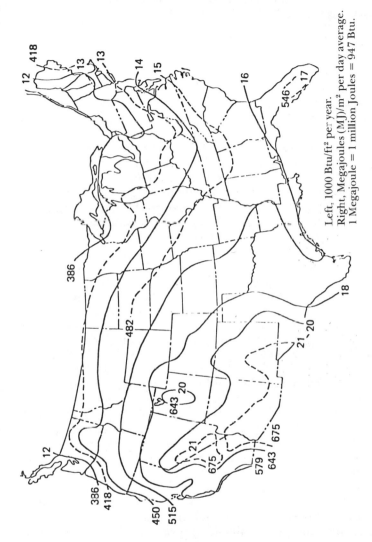

Figure 5.1 *Annual Total Solar Radiation, United States*

Source: NOAA Environmental Data Service, National Climate Center, Ashville, N.C.

Left, 1000 Btu/ft² per year.
Right, Megajoules (MJ)/m² per day average.
1 Megajoule = 1 million Joules = 947 Btu.

Btu/ft²/hr) is diminished, of course, by cloud cover or dust and smoke in the air; Arizona, however, is in the part of the country where the maximum levels of solar radiation are reached more often than elsewhere in the United States.

Climatic Factors

Arizona is a state with drastic extremes of climate. Because of the abrupt changes in altitude caused by the rugged Arizona terrain, the climate ranges from severe deserts to cool pine forests. Heating degree days (HDD) and cooling degree days (CDD), which are measures of how often and by how much during an average year the temperature falls below (HDD) or exceeds (CDD) some arbitrary temperature judged to be necessary for human comfort, yield standards in the United States of 65°F for heating and 75°F for cooling. Thus, on a day when the average temperature is 80°F, five cooling degree days would be accumulated, while on a day with a 60°F average temperature, five heating degree days would be amassed. The state has been separated into four zones on the basis of the heating and cooling needs imposed by the local climate. The zones vary from one in which cooling is never needed while heavy heating demands are present, to one in which moderate heating needs are combined with heavy cooling requirements. Flagstaff is the major city in the former zone, while Phoenix, Tucson, and Yuma all fall in the latter.

Opportunities to use solar energy in active and passive design techniques and energy-efficient approaches to resource management exist in all of the climatic zones of the state. Specific solar applications and building techniques will differ in Flagstaff and Yuma, naturally, but the vast majority of Arizonans live in areas where heating can be a minor or non-existent problem, while cooling is a major concern. The need for cooling is brought about by the high levels of solar insolation, from which it follows that the population centers where residences, businesses, and industry are concentrated are also the areas where abundant solar energy is available for use in solving the resulting energy problems.

The collector and storage systems must then be considered together during design in order to optimize the economic aspects of the application. Only a study of the integrated collector/storage system can clearly establish the cost of useful energy and what system tradeoffs are cost-effective. Since collectors usually dominate the total system cost, the extra collector area alone could more than offset the savings offered by cheaper, less efficient storage.

Solar Collectors

The various types of solar collectors extant with present technology can be grouped into four major categories; these are: 1) non-concentrating (or "flat plate"); 2) concentrating; 3) photovoltaic; and 4) hybrid. The first three of these categories are described below. A hybrid system is one which produces more than one type of energy, e.g., thermal and electrical, simultaneously.

Non-Concentrating

The flat plate collector is the most widely used type, and water most often is the working fluid. The basic collector consists of an absorber, glazing, insulation, and a frame. The working fluid is heated as it is passed over, under, or through the absorbing surface. More expensive models may contain special surface coatings designed to maximize the amount of sunlight they absorb and minimize the energy lost by reradiation at the operating temperature of the collector.

Successful implementation of solar-powered absorption refrigeration in residential applications may depend heavily on the development of economical flat plate collectors which, by using selective surfaces, will be able to provide the higher temperatures needed for absorption cooling.

The surfaces of these collectors are covered on the back and sides by standard types of insulation (e.g., Fiberglas), and enclosed on the front by one or two layers of glass or plastic. Several common materials, such as most glasses, are nearly transparent to visible light from the sun but absorb the infra-red reradiation from the absorber. (This is the basis of the "greenhouse effect" that overheats closed cars and rooms with southern exposures.)

Flat plate collector technology is well developed, and efficient high-quality collectors with maintenance-free lifetimes exceeding ten years are readily available on the open market.

Concentrating

Collectors of the concentrating type intercept large areas of the sun's rays and redirect them onto a smaller area at the focus of the instrument. They achieve considerably higher energy densities, and thus can provide higher-temperature working fluids. The energy density produced by a concentrating collector, divided by the density of the ambient solar radiation, is called the Concentration Ratio (CR) of the collector. CRs varying from a little over one to several thousand have been attained by current technologies. Three types of imaging concentrators are commercially available now. These are the Parabolic Trough Concentrator, the Compound Parabolic Concentrator (with or without vacuum tube receivers), and the Fresnel Lens.

Parabolic Trough Concentrators, the most widely used concentrating type, have been used successfully in many applications where mid-range heat (temperatures between about 212°F and 650°F) is needed. A 150 kw electrical generator, used to power irrigation pumps on the Dalton Cole Farm near Coolidge, is run by a field of such collectors, and a wide variety of industries, ranging from canning factories to textile operations, also have made successful use of them. Parabolic troughs have also been used for a variety of residential applications in the Southwest.

The Compound Parabolic Concentrator is capable of achieving CRs up to about 10; this is a low mid-range performance, but still well above the temperatures normally achieved by flat plate collectors. Moreover, this system lends itself to simple wind-resistant designs, such as the floating Carousel Collector developed at the University of Arizona. It is most effectively utilized in conjunction with a receiver that is enclosed in an evacuated tube to reduce convective losses from the hot absorber.

The Fresnel Lens Concentrator collectors provide CRs of around 40. Small circular lenses of the type that it uses are often used to concentrate solar radiation on photovoltaic cells in order to enhance their output. This type of device has been proposed for the 225-kw solar electrical system planned for the Phoenix Sky Harbor Airport by Arizona Public Service Company.

Photovoltaic

Photovoltaic (PV) collectors are normally referred to as a separate type, even though they too may be classified as a nonconcentrating or concentrating mode. In the latter case either a PV array, a thermal receiver, or both can be placed at the focus. PV cells operating at concentrated light levels must be cooled to maintain good performance, and usable thermal energy from the collector may be recovered from the cooling fluid. Such a system would fall in the hybrid category, combining both thermal and direct electrical production in one collector.

PV cells are too expensive today to be used for electrical

generation except in remote areas. Their potential is so great, however, that the federal government has instituted a development program in an effort to make PV arrays economic by 1990. Drastic cost reductions have already come about as a result of increasing volume and technological advances, causing a device that cost $30 per peak watt in 1976 to reach $8.00 per watt in 1978 (1975 dollars). A further reduction to $2.00 per watt (1975 dollars) in 1982 is the current goal.

The Solar Photovoltaic Energy Research, Development and Demonstration Act of 1978 provides for an accelerated development program to make PV technology cost-competitive with the conventional utility electric generator. Since, in addition, the Public Utility Regulatory Policy Act of 1978 requires utilities to pay a fair and equitable rate for excess electricity generated by user-owned systems, many interesting PV applications may surface in the coming years. As PV devices gain wider use, converting PV derived power to utility grids and determining the value of the excess energy are sure to raise major technical, legal, and political problems. Experiments, hard ware demonstration projects, and development of system models will have to occur before user-owner PV systems can be widely developed and accepted by utilities. Solar, thermal, wind, PV, cogeneration, and other alternate electrical generators are all covered by the Act, so its effects may prove to be quite widespread.

A number of PV flat plate modules, consisting of some thirty to forty individual solar cells interconnected to provide common voltages and mounted on a single panel, are available commercially for prices on the order of $10 for each peak watt available from the array. Such arrays are already in wide use in remote areas to power radio-telephones, microwave repeater stations, and the like. Concentrating arrays are undergoing widespread development, but have yet to be commercialized to the same extent as flat plate arrays.

In concentrator systems, such as the one being developed by the Sky Harbor project, a Fresnel lens or some concentrating mirror configuration is used to focus the sunlight onto one or more solar cells. Present systems using silicon cells have CRs in the range from 10 to 100; less common are high concentration systems using gallium arsenide cells with CRs around 1000.

The primary advantage of concentrator systems is that they replace expensive cell area with less expensive lens or reflector area, and so use fewer solar cells. For example, one cell with an optical concentration ratio of about 80 can produce 40 watts, while with no concentration, a flat plate module with at least thirty-three cells is needed to produce the same power.

Solar Use Sectors

Arizona's energy needs currently are met from four primary sources: petroleum, natural gas, coal, and generated hydroelectric power. From a technological point of view, conventional fuels could be replaced by solar energy in some portion of most end-use sectors: large-scale electric generation by central "power towers," industrial process heat requirements, and domestic hot water and space heating are all areas in which solar energy could make a significant contribution to the state's expanding energy needs. In particular, low-temperature (up to 350°F) thermal needs now being met by natural gas account for nearly all of the gas used in the residential and commercial sectors, and for a major portion of industrial and agricultural uses—in all some 45 percent of the natural gas in the state, or about 10 percent of the total energy used. Assuming future improvements in solar technologies make direct electrical generation feasible, the solar contribution could become significantly greater. Moreover, as the prices of exhaustible fossil fuels rise while the cost of solar declines, solar should become increasingly attractive in a variety of uses. The speed with which these developments will occur is subject to considerable uncertainty, of course.

In spite of propelling forces from applications like these, and the substantial state and federal tax credits available, serious restraining forces also exist. They include current building and zoning codes, high capital costs, artificially low costs of natural gas, and large numbers of existing energy-inefficient buildings with high retrofitting costs. Each major problem must be addressed and at least partly resolved before solar energy can begin to achieve its full potential in Arizona.

One problem is that conventional thinking often considers only the initial cost of a building and ignores the future expenses incurred by the eventual owner. To determine whether to choose solar options as capital investments, a relatively new way of studying costs needs to be applied—life-cycle costing. This costing concept looks beyond the initial payment for a product to the dollars that will be needed over its lifetime to cover financial charges (interest and amortization), operating costs, and maintenance. A long-term investment that achieves immediate energy cost savings may result in lower monthly costs over the life-cycle if all utility, maintenance, and mortgage costs are combined.* Such a product would tend to maintain a higher appraisal value, in addition to lower operating costs. Figure 5.2

---

*The comparisons should be made in dollars of comparable value, i.e., future savings and expenditures should be discounted at an appropriate rate to their present value. Simple calculations of payback periods yield similar results only for very short-time horizons and low discount rates.

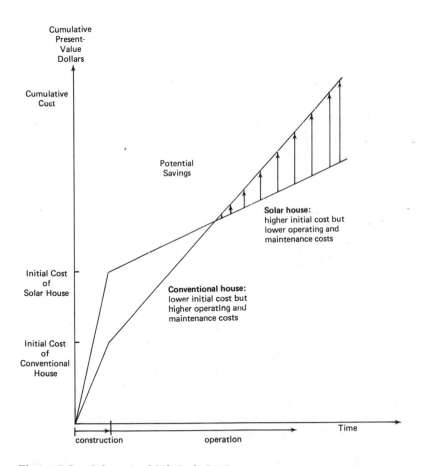

Figure 5.2 *Schematic of Life Cycle Costing*
Comparison of the cumulative costs of a solar and a conventional house, showing the greater future savings that can be had as a result of energy conservation and a properly designed home.

Note: Not drawn to scale.

illustrates the idea in schematic form, by comparing a conventional house that has a lower initial cost and higher operating costs with an energy-efficient solar home of similar size. Investors normally demand low initial costs for their projects, however, and prefer to let the consumer pick up future operating costs. This is especially true for commercial ventures, such as shopping centers, where operating costs may be passed on to the consumer in the form of higher prices for goods and services. Even for residences, as long as mortgage rates are at current high levels, very large fuel savings are required to overcome the increased initial cost of solar installations.

Residential and Commercial

In the United States, 33 percent of the total energy used is consumed by residential and commercial buildings. About 80 percent of this amount is used to heat, cool, and light buildings, the rest to power various appliances and water heaters.[1] Moreover, buildings are a long-term investment; those built fifteen years ago, when oil was $2.00 a barrel, will continue to stand if and when oil reaches $50.00 a barrel. It is essential, therefore, that new buildings be designed to reflect the increased costs of energy. Moreover, it is highly desirable to retrofit the many existing buildings that will still be in use in the year 2000. But active solar devices should only be used after the easiest energy-conserving steps have been taken. These include: orienting new buildings properly, designing them specifically for the climate, weatherizing new and existing buildings, and developing means of managing energy use within them to maximize energy-saving potentials.

Residential Within the residential sector, energy conservation plus solar energy utilization should be able to provide all the heating needs for new single-family and multi-family homes and apartments in the low desert regions of Arizona. The combination of heating and cooling in the same system, such as the use of rockbed storage for heat in the winter and coolness in the summer, improves the economics of solar buildings. In the higher regions, energy use in properly designed and managed homes could be reduced by 50 to 80 percent once costs of financing decline and natural gas prices are allowed to reach market levels.

As mentioned previously, solar energy use can be classified as either passive or active. Passive use involves the collection, storage, distribution, and, above all, control of solar energy through building design. Ideally, very little energy from additional sources would be required for heating or cooling. In such a system, energy flow may exist between the collector surface and storage, between the collector surface and the living space, or between storage and the living space. In direct-gain building types, solar radiation passes through the living space to the thermal mass, where it is stored for long-term heating. In essence the building is a "live-in" collector. In the indirect-gain type, the solar energy is stored in a thermal mass which subsequently transfers heat to the living space; the masonry Trombe wall, water Trombe wall,* and roof pond are three variations on this system. In the isolated-gain type of building, both collector and storage are thermally isolated from the living space, allowing more independent operation. Generally speaking, the passive approach is most appropriate in small buildings with simple layouts, but it can also provide significant advantages in the design of larger, more complex buildings.

Active solar systems utilize special mechanical and electrical equipment: solar collectors, heat storage elements, distribution and control systems—all of which require additional energy to operate. A primary advantage of such systems is the closer control of temperature that can be achieved by timing the delivery of solar heat to various parts of the living space. Moreover, active systems do not restrict building design by requiring that thermal storage masses be exposed directly to the sun.

Often a composite or hybrid approach is most cost-effective, as in a large building where spaces located adjacent to the exterior envelope are passively heated, while internal zones are actively conditioned. In residences, a passive system can be augmented by making use of fans to distribute solar heat more evenly, using the structure of the house itself as the thermal storage mass, and using an active system for water heating.

An interesting comparative example is provided in a recently completed study in which a local home builder constructed both a high-mass solar home and a standard low-mass control home with the same floor plan in the same area.[2] Both homes were heated during the day but, because of the stabilizing effect of the mass in the solar home, the temperature in it did not drop below 67°F at night; the auxiliary heat, set at 65°F, never came on. On the other hand, the occupants of the control home had to turn their furnace on every morning at 6:30, causing a large peak load to occur over a period of about 45 minutes. During particularly cold periods this peak load was repeated in the evenings. The solar home cost about 10 percent more than the other, but this kind of added cost can be substantially reduced as more such homes are built, and builders, subcontractors, and suppliers become more familiar with the products and construction techniques involved.

Low-rise, high-density apartment or townhouse developments generally use 25 to 50 percent less energy than suburban single-family houses.[3] It is worth emphasizing that these provide an exceptional opportunity for the application of passive solar

---

*A Trombe wall is a high-mass, south-facing wall with single or double glazing.

principles, because party walls between the units are often required to be solid concrete or masonry for sound isolation and
fire protection; such walls can be used advantageously as thermal masses.

Domestic water heating is the most widespread active solar
technology that can be considered fully cost-effective at the
present time. For most families the rising price of natural gas
and existing price of electricity, together with state and federal
tax credits, make possible a payback period for solar domestic
water heating systems of less than five years for electricity and
less than ten years for gas (these payback periods will become
shorter as interest rates decline and the cost of alternative energy sources rises). A more important consideration is that
a properly designed system can have total monthly payments
(including capital charges) that are actually lower than the cost
of the replaced conventional fuel, so that immediate operating savings are realized.

Solar installations for residential space heating in Arizona,
based on full costs of materials and labor, as of 1981 were not
competitive with natural gas, even with available tax credits.
However, natural gas prices may escalate rapidly in 1985, when
controls on prices of new natural gas are scheduled to be removed. At that time, solar space heating and other solar applications which replace natural gas will probably become fully
cost-effective in a wide range of situations.

Photovoltaic residential systems remain largely a hope for the
future, despite the completion in Phoenix of outstanding demonstration projects like the John F. Long house, fully powered by
this means. The cost of the photovoltaic cells themselves is still
very high compared to conventional electrical power sources,
though the potential for technical advances which could substantially reduce their price does exist. As with active solar devices,
PV systems become economical only after the overall energy
needs have been minimized.

Much the same remarks apply to solar-powered refrigerated
air conditioning. Though examples do exist (e.g., the John
Yellot home in Phoenix and the Stuart Willoughby house
in Tucson), they are far more expensive to install than conventional systems—about $5000 as opposed to $500 per ton as
of 1981.

Commercial   The commercial sector is made up of wholesale
and retail trade and the various service industries such as hotels,
motels, hospitals, restaurants, and laundries; a detailed listing
can be found in categories 50 through 80 of the U.S. Government Standard Industrial Classification (SIC) Code.[4] The major
portion of the energy consumed in this sector is used for heating
interior spaces and potable water supplies. Consequently, the
great potential of solar energy for space heating, plus its proven

potable hot water technology which is commercially available now, make this sector an ideal area for solar applications. The commercial sector accounted for 15 percent of the total Arizona consumption of natural gas in 1981, virtually all of which could be replaced by solar energy. Even the higher water temperatures used in hotel kitchens, restaurants, and laundries, could readily be supplied by established solar technology.

The commercial sector used about 36 percent of the electrical energy consumed in Arizona in 1981. Direct use of solar-generated electricity could replace some of this consumption in hybrid systems where PV cells are used to power parasitic loads such as pumps and blowers. Also, as noted earlier, a limited number of refrigeration systems that can be powered by low-temperature heat sources, such as hot water at around 200°F, are commercially available. Broad acceptance of solar in the commercial sector, of course, will occur only when more clear-cut economic advantages can be demonstrated than at present.

Since the majority of the thermal energy usage in the commercial sector is for hot water production, storage of the hot water itself in insulated tanks would be the most practical, and should be the most widely used, method of thermal storage. Many businesses already have hot water storage facilities for use with their conventional heating systems. But these may be poorly insulated or too small, particularly in gas-fired heating systems where recovery times are fast and large storage capacity has meant an unnecessary extra expense. To work satisfactorily, a solar installation may have to begin by adding both insulation and additional storage capacity.

One example of how much conventional fuel solar energy could replace in specific applications, is the hotel-motel industry, a major industry in Arizona. Energy use in hotels and motels falls into four primary categories: (1) hot water for guest rooms and kitchen use, (2) indoor and outdoor lighting, (3) heating, ventilating, and air conditioning (HVAC), and (4) "other," including gas or electric cooking and the powering of pool equipment and small appliances.

Table 5.1 summarizes information obtained during an in-depth energy audit of a large Tucson hotel. Examination of the data reveals that the major portion of the energy consumed is independent of the season, and varies little with the occupancy rate. The rate exception is space heating. Between 40 percent and 60 percent of total energy use is for hot water for guest rooms, the kitchen, and other facilities. Since delivered water temperatures range from 120°F in the guest rooms to 180°F in the kitchen, solar energy would be especially well-suited to replace present sources—primarily natural gas—in these applications.

Solar water heating also has been found to be practicable for

Table 5.1   *Energy Uses for a 200-Room Tucson Hotel Complex*

	Readily Replaceable by Solar		Not Readily Replaceable by Solar		Total	Estimated Readily Percentage Replaceable[c]
	Guest Room Hot Water	Other[a]	HVAC[b] Lighting (Million Btu)			
January	739.7	472.0	1,171.0	137.6	2,520.3	40.6
July	739.7	477.0	363.2	137.6	1,717.5	59.7
			(Per Cent)			
January	29.7	18.7	46.5	5.5	100.0	
July	43.1	27.8	21.1	8.0	100.0	

[a]Includes kitchen and facilities hot water which is not occupancy dependent.
[b]Heating, ventilating, and air conditioning.
[c]Guest room hot water plus 60% of "other."
Source: W. T. Snyder and F. W. Symonds, *Energy Audit of the Hilton Hotel,* Tucson, 7 April 1976, University of Arizona Systems Engineering Program.

carwashes and laundromats, where large quantities of moderately hot water are needed during the day. In one commercial carwash in Arizona, electrical energy use was reduced 90 percent after solar collectors were installed.

Other commercial buildings such as offices and schools, used only during the daytime, could be designed to coast through the night on stored warmth or coolness. During times of special cooling need, storage reservoirs could be recharged at night when off-peak power rates are in effect.

The larger the volume of a building, the less important climate becomes as a factor, because the exterior environment only directly affects its outside envelope. For large structures, energy management becomes the most useful technique. Awareness of a commercial building's energy use pattern can lead to dramatic savings. Department stores, for example, normally are built as hermetically sealed "black boxes" on the assumption that daylight would damage merchandise. Large amounts of artificial lighting must then be introduced to illuminate displays, creating a heat load that requires year-round air conditioning. Careful architectural design, as in many other cases in the commercial sector, could change this pattern entirely. Recent estimates have indicted that cost-competitive commercial structures could be designed with a 50 percent savings in fuel.

Industrial

The bulk of energy consumption in the industrial sector in Arizona is for process heat. Most of the electrical usage is in the high-temperature range (1000°F to 2000°F) required in smelting and refining; however, approximately 66 percent of the energy used for process heat is supplied by natural gas. Thus, solar energy could displace a major share of natural gas, plus some distillate fuel oils. Table 5.2 gives the top thermal energy consumers* in Arizona by three-digit SIC code.** It will be seen that

Table 5.2 *Arizona Industrial Thermal Energy End-Use Requirements, 1977*

Rank	SIC Code	Classification	Energy Use (Trillion Btu)	Under 212°F	212°F to 350°F	Over 350°F
				Thermal Energy End-Use Requirements (Trillion Btu)		
1	333	Primary Non-ferrous Metals	28.4	1.2	0	27.2
2	327	Concrete, Gypsum & Plaster Products	1.88	0.63	0.98	.27
3	335	Non-ferrous Rolling & Drawing	1.0	0	0.25	0.75
4	289	Miscellaneous Chemical Products	0.6	0	0.45	0.15
5	207	Fats and Oils	0.5	0.03	0.34	0.13
6	364	Electronic Components, Accessories	0.3			
7	201	Meat Products	0.3	0.294	0	0.006
8	295	Paving/Roofing	0.2	0	0.192	0.008
9	203	Preserved Fruits/ Vegetables	0.2	0.154	0.034	0.012
10	205	Bread and Other Bakery Products	0.2	0.024	0	0.175
11	208	Beverages	0.2	0.06	0.08	0.06
12	344	Fabricated Struc. Metal Products	0.1	0	0	0.1
13	202	Dairy Products	0.1	0.086	0.002	0.012
14	243	Millwork, Plywood, Struc. Membs.	0.1	0.05	0.05	0
15	275	Commercial Printing	0.1			
16	366	Communications Equipment	0.1			

Source: Energy Management and Policy Analysis Group, University of Arizona, *Survey and Analysis of Solar Energy Process Heat Opportunities in Arizona,* Engineering Experiment Station, University of Arizona, 1979.

*In addition to thermal uses, industrial energy is consumed for such purposes as on-site transportation and power, lighting, and air conditioning.
**The industries covered by these data account for 102.5 trillion Btu, or about half the total industrial energy consumed in Arizona in 1977 (excluding agriculture).

primary non-ferrous metals (copper, molybdenum, etc.) account for the bulk of thermal energy used by industrial plants in Arizona.

The greatest potential for solar thermal process energy exists in the temperature range below 212°F. Thermal energy in this range amounts to 2.6 trillion Btu—about 7 percent of the thermal energy and 2.5 percent of the total energy required by the industrial sector surveyed. Applications in the temperature range from 212°F to 350°F are the next most promising, totaling around 2.5 trillion Btu. Considering all thermal-process heat requirements below 350°F, solar energy has the potential to displace about 14 percent of the thermal industrial energy usage surveyed.

A prime consideration in the application of solar energy to industrial process heat is the cost competitiveness of the delivered energy. The average price per million Btu of gas sold to industrial users in Arizona in April 1981 was $2.61, which was $1.13 lower than the average for the Middle Atlantic states, and $2.20 below that of New England. The lower the conventional fuel costs, the more difficult the implementation of industrial solar applications becomes. Process heat in industry is often supplied in the form of process steam, although in many applications direct heating is used (e.g., electrolytic refining, reverberatory furnaces, kilns, etc.). Thus the suitability of solar (as well as cogeneration and geothermal energy) to industrial process heat application becomes a function of the process, process temperatures, and the cost of the conventional fuel to be displaced.

As noted above, the primary fuel used in Arizona for process heat is natural gas, with backup provided by fuel oil. During the mid-1970s, when natural gas was in short supply and large industrial users were severely curtailed, many firms converted their boilers to dual-fired (natural gas and fuel oil) systems. The gas supply situation has eased in the past two years, but the prospect of sharp price increases emphasizes the importance of solar application in many industrial uses.

As with buildings, solar systems in most cases would have to be retrofitted, and retrofitting implies additional costs. Some of the problems are: reinforcement of existing structures to accommodate the additional load of collectors; disruption of plant operations; various states of obsolescence of older facilities, making additional capital investments questionable; and reduced energy efficiency of older plants. All of these are significant but not necessarily insurmountable problems to the implementation of solar process heat. The ideal case, of course, would be to incorporate a solar energy system into a new plant design, or at least to make provision for easy retrofitting at some future date.

Specific Industrial Applications   When industrial subgroups in Table 5.2 are combined into two-digit groupings, the largest energy-consuming industries in the under-350°F range are stone, clay, and glass products (1.6 trillion Btu); primary metals (1.5 trillion Btu); and food and kindred products (1.1 trillion Btu).

The entire stone, clay, and glass products industry can be characterized as the manufacture of products by the application of heat in a kiln. Most of these require temperatures in excess of 1000°F in their main processes; however, the concrete, gypsum, and plaster products industries utilized 0.88 trillion Btu's, or roughly 25 percent of the total thermal energy used in this category at the last accounting. This ranks it as the second largest thermal energy consumer among these industries in Arizona, and identifies it as an industry with highly significant solar displacement potential.

The primary metal industries utilize about 24 percent of all industrial process heat under 350°F in Arizona. However, process heat constitutes only a small fraction of the total energy required to manufacture copper. The major portion of energy required is for machinery, transportation, and other electrical and mechanical equipment. The copper industry in Arizona does not dry the copper concentrate prior to smelting; but solar pre-drying of concentrate could provide a significant energy use reduction. The potential exists to displace about 1.4 trillion Btu/yr of conventional fuel, representing approximately 4 percent of the total thermal energy use in the industrial sector.

The electrolytic refining process utilizes process heat in the under-350°F range for the heating of electrolytic solutions. The solutions are constantly maintained at 140°F to 170°F, which requires about 4.34 million Btu/ton of refined copper for heating, usually by natural gas or fuel oil. The potential application of solar to this process is also very promising.

The food industries consume about 22 percent of the thermal energy in the under-350°F range, and while the percentage of the cost of any food product attributable to energy is relatively small, low profit margins make any decrease in the cost of energy attractive, provided initial costs of solar installations can be handled.

Agricultural

Agriculture in Arizona, as a consolidated business, constitutes the third largest industry in the state. Energy use in this sector includes all direct energy inputs that are devoted to cultivating the soil, raising livestock, or producing crops. Certain related commercial operations will also be included in the present discussion, specifically the initial processing of field crops (such as cotton ginning) and other commercial crop drying operations, dairying, livestock feedlot operations, and processing steps associated with egg production. Applications of solar energy to meet farm residence heating and cooling demands are similar to those for other residential or commercial buildings and will not be considered in this section.

Total energy use in the agricultural sector, as defined above, amounts to approximately 24 trillion Btu/yr, or about 3.5 percent of Arizona's overall energy use; Figure 5.3 provides details. Thermal energy uses account for about 5 percent of the agricultural total, and almost 93 percent of this is concentrated in three major processing operations: feed processing in beef cattle feedlots, cotton drying prior to ginning, and washing processes in dairies. Drying of field crops other than cotton accounts for about 6 percent of the total. The processes for each of these categories are characterized by relatively low temperature requirements, in the range from about 120°F to 210°F. Water, air, and steam are all used as delivery media.

Irrigation energy requirements within the state are so significant that they deserve special mention. Such use does not specifically fall under the heading of thermal process energy usage, but both thermal cycles and photovoltaic systems possess great potential for this area. Figure 5.3 shows that by far the largest energy requirement in the agricultural sector, is for crop irrigation pumping. For a typical cotton farm in Pinal County, irrigation energy demands may account for as much as 95 percent of the total on-farm energy use. Currently, there are a variety of demonstration projects and preliminary application efforts underway, such as the Coolidge project mentioned previously.

One of the more promising uses for solar energy is the preprocessing of feeds for feedlots. The effect of this processing is an enzyme breakdown which dramatically increases the grain's digestibility by the cattle that feed on it. A typical feedlot with about a 22,000-head capacity conducts this processing eight hours a day, 365 days a year. This coincides quite well with expected solar energy availability; it establishes the maximum possible yearly load factor with respect to the solar system's operation and minimizes the need for storage. Temperature requirements for appropriate steam generation are in the 200°F to 215°F range, which is at the upper limit of effective flat plate design capability.

Cotton is by far the most important of the field crops grown in Arizona, accounting for about 50 percent of Arizona's total crop value.[5] Process heat is required in the final step of the agricultural cotton production chain, the ginning process used to separate the lint cotton from the seed and chaff picked up at harvest. Drying is the first step in the ginning process. Typically, a 7 percent moisture content is considered desirable at the input

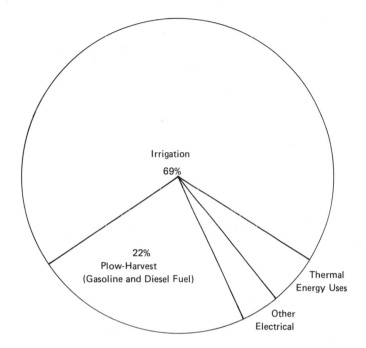

Figure 5.3 *Energy Use in Arizona Agriculture, 1977*

Source: University of Arizona, Engineering Experiment Station, 1979.

point to avoid equipment damage and optimize efficiency, while the average moisture content of cotton delivered to the gin site can range from 15 to 23 percent.

Moisture removal is accomplished in two continuous process steps. Field grade cotton is first fed into a cylindrical drying bin where hot air, supplied from a natural gas-fired burner, is used to provide initial moisture content reduction. Then the cotton is fed into vertical rack dryers to complete the process, but since the moisture content is lower at this point, the temperature of the drying air is usually lower also. The technical feasibility of drying the cotton using solar-heated air poses no real problem. The air temperatures in question (150°F to 200°F) are well within the capabilities of currently available solar systems.

In 1978 there were approximately 642,000 laying hens on Arizona's egg farms. Total output amounted to about 140 million eggs. A typical egg laying house is an environmentally-controlled structure with no windows, and interior lighting is scheduled to maximize productivity. This results in an elimination of space-heating requirements at most times throughout the year, with a corresponding increase in ventilation and cooling requirements. Brooding operations, on the other hand, are not common within the state.

Additionally there is a good potential for the use of solar energy in certain processing operations conducted on a typical egg farm. All eggs must be washed prior to packaging for delivery to purchasers. Mechanized washing operations require water at temperatures up to 180°F while actual washing is performed at about 115°F—the 180° water being used to maintain washer tank temperature through a closed-loop heat exchanger. Here again, the process requirement is the heating of water in a range that is a prime candidate for the application of solar energy.

Central Power Generation

The utility industry is becoming increasingly involved in solar energy applications and is seriously considering the use of central power installations using both PV cells and thermal electrical generation. The central station conversion of solar energy to electricity, and possibly to transportable fuels, represents a large potential application for solar energy in Arizona. However, the variability of the solar source and its low energy density raise major technical and economic difficulties. Even when modern planned technologies for solar-electric conversion become economically viable, the need for conventional plants to stand by for the night and during extended cloudy periods will probably limit solar plant penetration in total generating capacity.

Serious implications for land-use policy and environmental quality are sure to arise as a result of the large areas that would have to be provided for collector fields in solar central power stations. Arizona Public Service Company's (APS) solar repowering project at its Saguaro Station, for instance, requires over 500 acres of land for the 10,500 heliostats needed. Sunbelt areas will be at some advantage in that land is more plentiful in the West, but land use is of high interest to many groups in all parts of the country.

Nevertheless, solar-electric generation does represent a possible alternative to dependence on expensive generation by oil or gas-fired plants. In Arizona, oil and gas are used to meet peaking loads and certain intermediate loads, especially during summer afternoons and evenings. Solar-electric generation may be suited for this application.

More complicated procedures of converting sunlight into thermal energy, before converting it into electricity, may become competitive sooner than direct conversion. While energy in a working fluid heated in a solar collector, such as a Flat Plate, Trough or Point Concentrator, can be converted to electricity in conventional turbomachinery, the economics of solar generation often improve as the efficiency increases with the high temperatures produced by higher concentration.

In one concept, noted earlier, fluid is heated in a receiver atop a tall tower surrounded by a field of tracking mirrors, called heliostats, that reflect sunlight to the top of the tower. The heated fluid is then used in a steam or gas turbine to produce electricity, or stored for later use. Several such central power receiver system designs have been developed. They range from conventional water/steam technology to advanced technologies utilizing molten salt, liquid sodium, air and helium transfer fluids, and solar/fossil fuel hybrid techniques. The latter system is directed towards increasing the availability of the plant when the sun is not shining by the use of a fossil fuel like coal; when combined with a storage capability, it may be uniquely applicable to the Southwest, as it can provide an annual availability up to 92 percent (assuming the economics ultimately justify such an application).[6]

Cost has been the driving force in delineating the available options for solar central receiver plants. The water/steam central receiver option will be demonstrated first in 1982 at a 10 Mw pilot plant under construction near Barstow, California. This plant represents first generation solar technology and will not be competitive with plant efficiencies that can be obtained using present-day steam turbine techniques. It is not considered to be a cost-competitive design, but is designed to demonstrate that the central receiver system is technically viable and that all subsystems are functional.

Additional prospects are offered by hybrid solar-oil/gas-fired plants. In the repowering mode, a solar thermal plant is placed adjacent to an existing oil/gas-fired plant and used to generate steam for the existing plant's turbines when solar energy is available, thus displacing conventional fuels. Such designs may be capable of both stimulating industrial production of solar components and giving utilities the confidence to proceed with stand-alone solar power plants. This arrangement may create a heliostat production base which, in turn, would result in reducing their cost, currently representing over 70 percent of the capital cost of a solar plant. Such a development would mean significant oil import savings to the nation.

One example of such an approach is the 100 percent "repowering" plan for the Arizona Public Service Company's 115-Mw Saguaro Station near Tucson, an intermediate-to-peaking facility. The company's analysis—based on a field of 10,500 heliostats, four hours of thermal storage in molten salt,

and retention of a dual/solar conventional fuel capability—
indicates projected oil and gas saving of 342,000 barrels, equivalent to about $9.7 million yearly at 1980 prices. Estimated
capital costs of the solar unit are about $210 million.

Central station generation by photovoltaic arrays also is a
distinct technical possibility. This mode of operation offers
a number of attractions. First, the fuel is free, with no delivery
costs. Second, because of their relative simplicity, photovoltaic
power plants can be built quickly and be ready to start delivering
electricity within perhaps two years from the start of a project;
this would significantly reduce interest costs during construction. Also, the modularity of such plants lends itself to construction in sections, with each section becoming capable of
producing power as soon as it is added. Third, a solar photovoltaic power plant, as a utility would use it, should not have
damaging environmental effects. Finally, although there are
some economics of scale, the optimum size of PV power plants
is fairly small, compared to conventional generating units—
probably in the 10 to 100 Mw range. These factors give PV
power plants great siting flexibility, including the ability to
locate near the load, and potential advantages in smaller
markets (assuming PV costs come into economic range).

The variability of the solar resource reduces the effective capacity of any solar electric generator as a reliable generating
plant. Solar electric generation, especially solar thermal-electric
generation, will become competitive first with oil and gas-fired
generating plants used to provide short-duty (peaking and intermediate) cycles. Although through the use of solar/fossil/
storage hybrids it is technically possible to design high-capacity
plants for base load applications, economics will probably continue to favor coal and nuclear plants for the majority of electrical generation for the foreseeable future.

Institutional and Financial Constraints to Solar Applications

The public is becoming increasingly aware of solar energy, but
often does not have enough specific information to make informed decisions. While performance information on collectors
has been available, for example, results on the operation of
complete systems have not been standardized, and performance
information on such systems is not now readily available.[7]

In spite of information gaps, solar installations in Arizona are
increasing rapidly. The Arizona Solar Energy Commission estimates that while in 1978 only 3,000 solar systems existed in the
state, by 1981 there were approximately 30,000.[8] During this

same period, educational efforts by state and federal organizations and private enterprise have also grown significantly.

Building codes which do not adequately address solar energy uses may adversely affect the developing solar industry. Of the over 10,000 municipal building codes in the country, only a handful make provisions for solar energy.[9] When codes do not include solar energy, disincentives are created. The processing of applications for variances for solar installations, for example, creates uncertainty, delays, and additional expenses. Even if codes do address solar uses, they may set such strict controls that costs are substantially increased.

Recognizing the need for providing solar energy uses in local building codes, the Department of Energy commissioned the Council of American Building Officials to develop a national code manual. The council's report was recently published, and the City of Tucson is already considering incorporating the recommended provisions into its building code. Many Arizona communities have also adopted, or are currently considering adopting, model plumbing provisions which relate to solar. Twenty-three Arizona communities, for example, were represented at a May 1981 training session which focused on such a model.[10]

Lack of trained, qualified installers also has been a major problem. The solar market has grown so fast that it has outstripped the pool of qualified installation personnel. To alleviate this situation, solar trade organizations have joined with the Maricopa Technical Community College to set up a solar technician training and certification program. In addition to increasing the supply of trained installers, it is hoped that certification by a joint state-builder program will help increase consumer assurances.[11]

Costs remain a major constraint to solar energy. Even with generous state and federal tax credits, active solar systems require high initial capital investments and have long payback periods. Solar, for example, was as of 1981 not competitive with natural gas; the planned 1985 decontrol, however, could force gas prices upwards and make solar competitive.

Hopes that life-cycle costing concepts would catch on with the public have not been realized thus far. A study on the acceptability of solar heating and cooling to home buyers in the Denver, Colorado, and the Philadelphia, Pennsylvania–Wilmington, Delaware, areas found most home seekers unwilling to incur larger monthly mortgage payments even though the increase would have been more than offset by fuel savings. The builders interviewed agreed. Consumers appeared to be more concerned with saving their monthly mortgage payments than with saving energy costs. Consumers may require more education before they accept higher mortgage payments in order to realize lower operating costs.

Passive solar, if incorporated into initial residential designs, not only involves small initial costs but also allows the installation of smaller and less expensive conventional heating and cooling equipment. Yet passive solar technology does not receive the same attention as active solar, perhaps because it has had fewer standard-bearers to promote it. As one report explains:

> Knowledge about passive solar systems has not been greatly developed outside the mainstream of the active solar field. In part this is due to the lack of a common interest base. The cause-oriented promotional and lobbying groups who have spurred public acceptance of solar energy for heating and cooling have often disregarded passive systems. More seriously, government-funded research and information-dissemination efforts have, at the time of this writing, consistently ignored passive solar technologies.[12]

Because passive solar is difficult to retrofit, it is more associated with building design than with specific item sales. Thus, the sales force for passive, which is composed mainly of the building industry and architects, is smaller than that for active solar, which includes a growing number of commercial firms.

Widespread on-site solar energy generation could have significant impact on traditional institutional arrangements for energy distribution. Decentralized energy systems, especially if they were to spread quickly, pose a potential threat to the stability of the established grid. At the very least they would require consideration of the changing role of utility companies with regard to their customer.

Individuals who incorporate passive or active solar systems may find their solar installation in the future shaded by a neighbor's building or vegetation. Arizona's relatively low-density communities and flat terrain make shading problems less serious than in areas where neighboring structures are located much closer or where the terrain is hilly. Moreover, state law has specifically directed that as of 1981, local communities consider solar access ordinances. A number of communities are investigating the form such ordinances could take.[13]

In addition, various restrictions designed to promote an aesthetically pleasing environment may conflict with a property owner's desire to utilize solar applications. These restrictions are of two general types: those imposed by private agreement in the form of restrictive covenants and those imposed by governmental bodies through zoning statutes and ordinances. Arizona has passed legislation which prohibits any new covenant or deed restriction or condition which would limit the installation or use of solar energy devices. However, the law does not affect any restriction or covenant enacted prior to the effective date of the law, 17 April 1980; a bill introduced during the 1981 legislative session that would have addressed the problem of pre-1980 restrictions did not pass. Existing restrictions thus remain a major constraint to solar usage in some areas of the state.

Chapter 6

Cogeneration and Distributed Energy Systems

Cogeneration may be broadly defined as the simultaneous generation of electricity or mechanical energy and useful heat. As recently as 1950, before low-cost natural gas became widely available, cogeneration accounted for approximately 15 percent of the nation's electrical power. By 1973, this percentage had declined to less than 5 percent, largely as a result of the ready availability of inexpensive energy. Cogeneration is an efficient energy technology but has not yet gained widespread use because of institutional obstacles and economic conditions which are being altered by rapidly rising fuel costs.

Cogeneration is also known by other terminology, in part depending on the situation in which it is used. "Total energy," "on-site power," and "energy cascade" are often used in connection with industrial–commercial operations, and "district heating" and "community energy systems" in connection with urban cogeneration, which is common in many European cities. Urban cogeneration is based on centralized power production and distribution, and is normally controlled by a private or public utility. When cogeneration takes place at the point of use, it can be characterized as a distributed system; on-site cooperation systems are often owned by the user but could be owned by a utility. The dispersed nature of both urban and rural activities in Arizona makes it more likely for decentralized cogeneration and small power production to become economically attractive rather than centralized cogeneration by a utility. Consequently, cogeneration by utilities is not discussed here.

Added interest in cogeneration is being provided by the Federal Public Utility Regulatory Policy Act (PURPA) of 1978, which was designed to encourage on-site cogeneration and small power production. The new law provides for special terms and rates for both the purchase and sale of electricity between utilities and cogenerators. Utilities are required to purchase excess electricity produced by cogenerators and small power producers at a price that equals the avoided cost to the utility. The avoided cost is construed to be the cost of generating the power itself or of purchasing it elsewhere.

Technical Considerations

To appreciate the potential value of the energy that resides in energy sources and fuels, one should first understand that energy forms vary in their ability to do work. A useful measure of energy utility is embodied in the concept of available work or thermodynamic availability. Availability provides a quantitative measure of energy and of quality as well. Thus, even though 1 kg of gasoline can be said to have the same energy content as 2.296 kg of water warmed to 5°C (9°F) above ambient, the form and quality of the energy are different. The gasoline has chemical energy and the water has thermal energy, and, more important, the ability of gasoline to perform useful work (for example, to drive an engine) is much greater. If the gasoline were burned with no losses and the heat liberated were used to warm some water, no energy would be "consumed" (though fuel would be); yet nearly all the potential to do work would be lost. Clearly, the work utility of tepid water is radically less; that is, the quality of the energy has been degraded. A better way to utilize the energy effectively and yet heat the water would be to use the gasoline first to drive an engine and then heat the water by cooling the engine and exhaust gases.

This procedure for heating the water exemplifies the basic concept of cogeneration. It is more energy-efficient to extract work from fuel in an engine, generating electricity, and then to undertake a heating process, rather than to perform each operation independently and in parallel. The bottom line for the application of cogeneration is the simultaneous need for mechanical or electrical power and thermal energy. In residential and commercial buildings, the need for electricity and space heating or absorption cooling could make cogeneration attractive for preplanned community systems. In industry, the requirement for plant electric power in conjunction with process heat, such as steam or hot air, makes cogeneration technically feasible and economically attractive in many situations. The economic justification for cogeneration, however, requires a constant and proper ratio between electric and heating demands at a given time, a ratio that is not always achieved in real situations, though careful load planning may help to do so. Most often in industrial situations, the requirements for process heat exceed those for electrical generation.

Many applications can be made economically viable with the supplementary sale of excess electricity or heat. One effect of PURPA is to enhance the sale of excess power by requiring that public utilities establish rate structures for the purchase of independently generated electricity, and that they not discriminate against or impede the establishment of such small generation facilities.

Industrial cogeneration and community energy systems could imply a trend toward more distributed energy systems rather than highly centralized power generation facilities. Furthermore, the introduction of low-cost solar photovoltaics and wind systems in the future may radically affect the mix of centralized versus decentralized power generation.

Technical Concepts

In most modern industrial and commercial applications, process heat is supplied in the form of steam or hot air from a boiler, and required electric energy is supplied by a central power plant that is often many miles away. Figure 6.1 shows three possible cogeneration alternatives. In System *A,* steam is produced by a conventional boiler at a temperature and pressure above that required by process heating. The steam is first fed through a turbine from which energy is extracted and used to drive an electric generator. Exhaust steam or intermediately extracted steam is used for heating purposes. In System *B,* fuel is supplied directly for the combustor of a gas turbine system which turns an electric generator. The hot turbine exhaust gases can then be used directly or indirectly to produce steam in an exhaust-heat boiler. System *C* employs a standard diesel engine-generator set to produce electricity with engine-exhaust and cooling-jacket heat recovered for direct heat use of steam production.

In the above cogeneration systems, total fuel utilization, i.e., the percentage of fuel energy productivity utilized in the process, can approach 80 percent, and a 30 to 40 percent fuel savings is possible.

In addition to cogeneration and small on-site electrical generation, the PURPA Act encourages the use of renewable energy sources. Renewables are basically derived from solar energy directly or indirectly; they include photovoltaics conversion, wind, and biomass. Combustible gases formed by the decomposition of municipal and agricultural waste also can be used to power engines or heat boilers. Many biomass projects are currently under way in numerous locations across the country.

Cogeneration and many of these renewable applications are likely to become increasingly attractive as fuel and electric

STEAM TURBINE TOPPING CYCLE

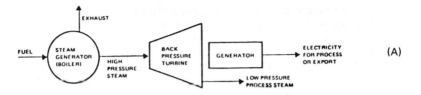

(A)

GAS TURBINE TOPPING CYCLE

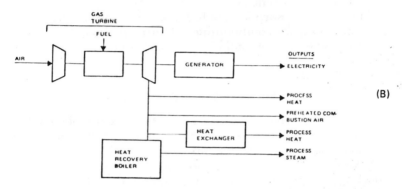

(B)

DIESEL ENGINE TOPPING CYCLE

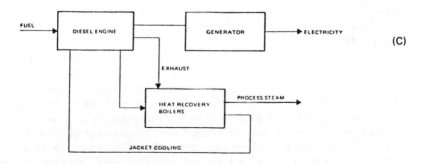

(C)

Figure 6.1   *Examples of Cogeneration Systems in Industrial Processes*

energy prices rise. Current advances with coal conversion techniques are also expected to enhance the prospects for suitable cogeneration projects.

The opportunities for cogeneration in Arizona industry include:

1. Mining and associated processing operations,
2. Concrete products manufacturing,
3. Processing of food, and related operations, and
4. Meat packing and cattle feed operations.

In the commercial building sector, some opportunities can be found in:

1. Hospitals and clinics,
2. University and college complexes,
3. Large shopping centers, and
4. Community centers.

The use of absorption cooling instead of mechanical-electric systems for space conditioning enhances the need for heat all year round in the hot southern part of the state, and would favor cogeneration.

Incentives and Barriers

The energy savings from cogeneration are not obtained free of charge. Combined cycles require more equipment, greater capital investment, and increased operating and maintenance costs. Reliability and load matching are other concerns in a practical application. If the facility is operated by a private user, backup electrical supply must be available for those times when the plant cannot deliver the demand. If the plant is operated as a public utility, a constant use for cogenerated steam is required. If a cogenerating company cannot use the steam for part of the day or year (because of seasonal or other production variations), the steam must be dumped, with a corresponding loss in efficiency.

From the user's point of view, a decision to cogenerate depends on technical and financial considerations. Moreover, there are a number of more subtle concerns which increase the complexity of activities and doing business, such as setting up additional operational infrastructures, incompatibility with the main line of business, and increased government regulation. In the past, low fuel and electricity prices have generally favored the use of on-site boilers for heat and purchased off-site electricity, except in some specialized situations. However, cogeneration has been popular in many chemical process industries, where the operation is just another subunit in a complex plant. The sale of surplus heat or electricity generally has not been a contingent requirement.

Increased energy costs and the potential to sell back surplus electricity are shifting the balance toward more cogeneration.[1] However, the appropriate situations will still remain few as long as a central utility can continue to provide the cheapest means of generated electricity. User-generated electricity, without some additional dual benefit or availability of a cheap alternative on-site fuel source is not competitive with central power production. Improved technology in the future, which permits the use of solar, wind, and bio-energy, will of course favor more on-site generation. Even with these there may be some question concerning who should appropriately own on-site generators: whether it should be the user, some external organization, or a public utility.

In the past, there has been little incentive for the sale of industrial cogenerated electric power because of the low buy-back prices offered by utilities. Electric utilities have also practiced some price discrimination in the rates they charge to cogenerators for standby electric power. From the utilities' viewpoint, the uncertain quantity and timing of cogenerators' demand for electricity warrants a higher charge, and thus they have treated standby charges as demand-related or capacity charges. The issue is whether the charges for providing service should be based on the full cost or a partial allocation, as in marginal costing.

Although utility pricing policies are crucial, the critical consideration in the investment decision of an unregulated firm is the need for a return on investment commensurate with the risks involved. For example: there are technical and financial risks associated with a new venture, and there is the risk of subjection to state and federal regulations affecting the production of electricity. The greater the uncertainty perceived by the industrial firm, the higher the discount rate used to evaluate future benefits and the lower the acceptable net present value of the investment will be. Further drawbacks to investment have been set forth by other investigators:

> Utility systems tend to draw low priority for investment purposes, simply because the criteria by which industrial performance is judged have little to do with utility expenditures. Established accounting procedures and tax laws do little to help the situation. Utility services which are purchased are fully tax-deductible operating expenses, whereas investments in utility systems are subject to long-term depreciation schedules.[2]

Even when technical conditions and fuel costs are favorable, discriminatory pricing practices by electric utilities or the state regulatory agencies, regulatory uncertainty, and tax disincentives can constitute added deterrents to on-site power production and cogeneration.

The Public Utilities Regulatory Policy Act (PURPA)

The PURPA Act of 1978 and subsequent Federal Energy Regulatory Commission (FERC) rulings of March 1980 are intended to relieve some uncertainties and enhance the benefits of cogeneration and small power production. The provisions are limited to qualifying facilities. Criteria for qualifying as small power production facilities include maximum size (80 Mw), fuel use (within a calendar year, no more than 25 percent may be fossil fuels*), and ownership (no more than 50 percent equity interest can be held by an electric utility or its affiliates). The essential features of the regulations are to exempt the qualifying facilities from certain regulatory controls normally applicable to public utility power plants which may have restricted tax benefits, oil and gas use, and environmental releases; and to oblige the state regulatory agencies to set rates for both the purchase from, and sale of electricity to, the qualifying facilities, based on calculated avoided power costs for each utility.

Large areas of discretion are reserved for the state regulatory authorities (e.g., Arizona Corporation Commission) in implementing these rules, particularly those associated with establishing rates. ACC adopted such rules on July 22, 1981; specific rates were required to be in place within days. In many states, favorable rates to encourage cogeneration have been in effect for many years. In California, the utilities have actively solicited and encouraged the buy-back of privately generated electricity; their motivation has been the limited power plant capacity to meet service area demands because of stringent environmental and state restrictions. To date, cogeneration with electricity return to the grid in Arizona has been insignificant. The Arizona Corporation Commission has implemented the PURPA rules and defined special cogeneration rates for each of the utilities. In addition, the Salt River Project, which does not come under the jurisdiction of the Commission, has taken steps toward establishing rates and standards for buying back power from industrial cogenerators.[3]

Utility Perspective

The public utilities' view toward cogenerated power is a natural business response to perceived competition and impact on revenues. The utility reaction may be favorable or not, de-

---

*The rules have been amended recently to allow diesel engines to qualify, although they are fired with fossil fuels.

pending on the local situation. In California, where the utilities have been buying imported power from other states (Arizona, for example), privately generated local on-site power is considered a desirable commodity and is therefore encouraged by favorable rates. In contrast, electric generating capacity available to Arizona's utilities is substantially greater than peak demand within the state and likely to remain so until 1990. Consequently, there is not imminent need for privately generated electricity in Arizona.

Aside from excess capacity, existing regulations offer a disincentive for cogeneration because the utility's allowable rate of return is calculated as a percentage of the utility's investment in plant and equipment. This formula encourages investment in owned generating plants but not in purchased power because such power does not enlarge the rate base. As one investigator has pointed out:

> There is no opportunity for leveraging unless there is an investment. The utility, over the long haul, succeeds by making new investments. If it merely marketed power produced by manufacturing firms, it would have fewer investment opportunities. It is therefore in its best interest to discourage any form of power generation.[4]

If the cogeneration site is very large, the demand for base load power from the larger plants could be affected. Such large-scale conversions to cogenerated power have occurred elsewhere, in the New York Consolidated Edison service area, for example, where electrical costs are double those of Arizona utilities.

Utility-User Connection

Another utility concern is the effect of interconnection between cogenerator and utility on the utility's statutory responsibility to provide reliable service. There are first some technical standards that must be adhered to by the cogenerator to ensure compatibility, safety, and reliability of the interconnected systems. These can generally be resolved with appropriate devices and hardware, whose cost is the responsibility of the cogenerator.

In addition, there are some system-related issues and costs. Normally, the cost imposed upon the utility system by the possibility that a cogenerator might demand service during a peak period would justify the charging of a relatively higher standby rate. However, PURPA's mandate of nondiscrimination toward cogenerators implies that this cost will be shared by all of the system's customers. Another possible interconnection problem is that the exported, cogenerated power will not always coincide with the load demand of the utility system. In other words, the cogenerator typically returns power when the utility does not need it, such as at night and on weekends. The utility, furthermore, must maintain control over the electric power entering the grid to ensure system stability and security.

It should be noted that much utility opposition to cogeneration could easily be dispelled by allowing utilities to take advantage of cogeneration, either as full owners or in joint ventures with industrial firms. With the utilities as an active partner, the number of opportunities for cogeneration would be augmented significantly because many of the institutional and technical constraints mentioned before, such as operation and maintenance, interconnection and load problems, would be alleviated.

According to some recent studies, as much as one-fifth of all energy consumed by American industry could be saved through cogeneration, although such estimates may reflect more the technical capabilities than existing economic and other conditions.[5] The potential may be further enhanced by advanced energy conversion technologies, such as the Sterling Engine, fuel cells, and current developments like the General Motors engine that combines steam and gas turbines.[6]

For Arizona, with its low population density and few large energy-using industries, cogeneration possibilities are limited but nonetheless significant. According to a 1981 University of Arizona study,[7] the potential is on the order of 300 Mw. Over 200 Mw of this is in the industrial sector, some 95 percent of it in industries involving nonferrous metals (chiefly copper and related products), but the list also includes a large number of relatively small industries. Commercial sector potential is estimated at 30 Mw and includes such establishments as laundries, hotels, shopping centers, hospitals, and food packing operations. Agricultural applications, estimated at 25 Mw, include crop drying, feed-lot operation, and cotton ginning. These estimates are based entirely on the technical characteristics of the sector study; no detailed economic studies had been executed as of 1981.

The Case for Cogeneration

Cogeneration can offer several important advantages over conventional electrical generation. It permits the productive use of valuable energy that might otherwise be wasted. As a result of higher operating efficiencies, there is a reduction in thermal and other pollutants (large pollution abatement facilities may, however, be more efficient). Furthermore, some cogeneration systems can operate on alternate fuel sources and thus permit the substitution of more abundant, lower-cost fuels for scarce oil and natural gas.

Widespread application of cogeneration throughout the United States could result in a significant level of energy savings. Department of Energy (DOE) studies estimate potential savings at 725,000 to 1,600,000 barrels of oil equivalent per day by 1985. These studies estimate that cogenerated power could produce up to 740 billion kwh of electrical energy in 1985.[8]

Cogeneration will be most attractive technically and economically in situations where there is active utility participation— ownership or operation. This conclusion is supported by DOE estimates that some 40 percent of U.S. cogeneration potential is not economical for industry alone without utility involvement. However, utilities are concerned with how cogeneration affects system availability and reliability, capacity expansion planning, and financial return, and with whether cogeneration can offer advantages related to compliance with environmental regulations.

Alternative, renewable energy sources offer more opportunities for on-site power generation. Although Arizona's excess centralized electrical capacity now retards the promotion of cogeneration and independent power production in the state, as energy prices escalate, the trend toward greater efficiency in energy use will undoubtedly favor expanding cogeneration.

Chapter 7
Geothermal Energy Resources

Geothermal energy is heat from the interior of the earth, and because it exists everywhere, it is perhaps the most abundant energy resource available to man. There is general agreement that if one could drill deep enough into the earth, to depths exceeding man's present ability, an inexhaustible quantity of heat energy would be available at any location. While current technology cannot tap and utilize these deep geothermal sources, there are numerous regions around the world where anomalous concentrations of useful heat occur at or near the earth's surface (less than 5000 meters [16,400 ft.]. Many of these areas are accessible and exploitable today.

Terminology and Classifications

The terminology used in this report was established by the U.S. Geological Survey (USGS) in Circular 790 (1979, p. 4). The USGS defined "useful accessible resource base," or *resource*, as "the thermal energy that could be extracted at costs competitive with other forms of energy at a foreseeable time, under reasonable assumptions of technological improvement and economic favorability." The resource concept was further divided into "identified" and "undiscovered" components. "Identified" refers to specific concentrations of geothermal energy known and characterized by drilling or by geochemical, geophysical, or geologic evidence. "Undiscovered" refers to unspecified concentrations surmised to exist on the basis of broad geologic knowledge and theory. In contrast, geothermal *reserve* was defined by the USGS as "that part of the geothermal resource that is identified and also can be extracted legally at a cost competitive with other commercial energy sources at present." For example, Yellowstone National Park contains a significant, identified geothermal resource. However, the area will never be included in the class of geothermal reserves because its status as a national park precludes legal extraction of the geothermal energy beneath the park. As another example, certain sites in the Imperial Valley of southern California also contain significant, identified geothermal resources, but are presently excluded from classification as geothermal reserves. Problems of scaling and corrosion caused by the heavy brines prevent these resources from being cost-competitive at present. Note that these definitions are independent of resource temperature; resources and reserves can have low as well as high temperatures.

There are three distinct ways to classify geothermal energy. The first method is based on temperature of the resource: <90° C (<194° F) = low temperature; 90–150° C (194–302° F)=moderate temperature; and >150°C (>302°F)=high temperature.

The second classification scheme is based on the fluid phase extracted from the reservoir, a classification especially useful to geothermal engineers. In this scheme there are three major divisions: first, the vapor-dominated system, characterized by steam only; second, the hydrothermal system, having a steam and hot water mix, or hot water only; and third, the hot dry rock system, having no fluid at all.

The third classification scheme separates geothermal systems according to the heat source producing the resource: whether it be a young magmatic intrusion; a recent intrusion of magma (i.e., less than 1 million years old) into the crust; a high heat flow; or a high concentration of radioactive elements (i.e., uranium, thorium, potassium).

All three classifications can be applied to a single resource; for example, The Geysers is a high-temperature, vapor-dominated system that has a magmatic heat source. Among the different types of geothermal systems that exist, vapor-dominated systems are the most desirable resources because clean, dry steam (steam without water) is the most economic and technically feasible way to generate electricity. However, these systems are extremely rare. Hydrothermal systems (hot water or hot water and steam mix) require more innovative technology, but have the advantage of often providing a hotter fluid (to 360°C [680°F]) than vapor-dominated reservoirs, which are typically about 230°C (446°F). Hydrothermal systems also comprise the low- to moderate-temperature systems used for direct-heat applications, and are now known to comprise the majority of geothermal occurrences worldwide.

Geologic Environments

Geothermal systems are mostly related to definite geologic features, most of which can be found in the United States. Along the Atlantic Coastal Plain and the Gulf Coast, thick sediments, some greater than 9,000 m (about 30,000 ft.) act as insulation, thereby trapping and storing the underlying heat energy. Areas of recent volcanism in northern New Mexico, the Cascade Range of the Pacific Northwest and northern California, and Hawaii exhibit significant and promising signs of geothermal energy. In some instances two or more geologic features occur in the same region, often resulting in vast reservoirs of geothermal energy. One such area is the Imperial Valley of southern California. The U.S. Geological Survey has estimated that six geothermal sites in the Imperial Valley together may be capable of producing 6,790 megawatts of electrical energy,[1] or almost half of the total electric generating capacity in Arizona in 1990.

Reservoir Sizes and Lifetimes

Frequently geothermal energy is regarded as a renewable resource, but that is not the case. Geothermal reservoirs have definite volumes and lifetimes. As individual wells in a given geothermal field decline in production, additional wells are required to maintain the supply of hot water or steam. The potential lifetime of a geothermal reservoir varies with each system. Generally a high-temperature reservoir must have an estimated producing life of at least thirty years to make it economical to develop the geothermal field and to build the electrical generating facility. Low- to moderate-temperature geothermal reservoirs must also have an estimated lifetime that makes the direct-use application economically feasible.

Geothermal reservoirs also have definite sizes or volumes, which vary greatly and have a direct bearing on reservoir life. The Yellowstone National Park area has an estimated reservoir volume of 1230 to 2410 km^3, with an average of 1,820 km^3 (43 to 85 million cubic feet with an average of 64 million cubic feet). Numerous small resources have reservoir volumes of 3 km^3 or less (106,000 cubic feet).[2]

Geothermal Energy in Arizona

Northeastern Arizona is part of the Colorado Plateau, a region of high elevation and nearly flat-lying sedimentary rocks. With the exception of a possible aquifer containing warm groundwater that could be used for low-temperature direct-heat applications, the probability of geothermal resources occurring beneath the Colorado Plateau appears minimal—except possibly for the areas around Sanders and Springerville–Alpine (Fig. 7.1).

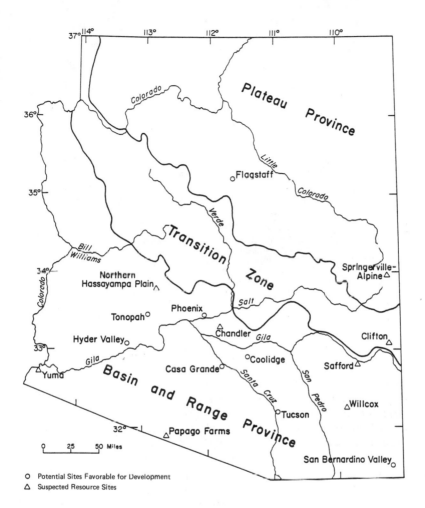

Figure 7.1 *Geothermal Resource Areas in Arizona*

Source: Arizona Bureau of Geology and Mineral Technology

The geothermal resources thus far identified in Arizona have mostly low to moderate temperatures, and are found mainly in the south-southwestern half of the state as a result of regional geologic structures (compare Fig. 7.1 with Fig. 3.4, *Arizona Energy*).[3]

The south-southwestern Arizona region is characterized by large blocks that have been either uplifted into mountain ranges or downdropped to create deep basins now filled with sediments (Fig. 7.2). The sediments are relatively poor conductors of heat,

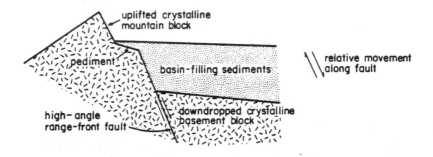

Figure 7.2   *Schematic Cross Section of Typical Basin, Basin and Range Province, Arizona*

Source: Arizona Bureau of Geology and Mineral Technology

and consequently act as insulation to trap the heat that occurs at depth and to prevent its dissipation at the surface. Where permeable sediments are water-saturated and deep (greater than 300 m or 985 ft), important low-temperature "undiscovered resources" (<90°C, or 194°F) may occur. In many cases, very deep fractures, which occur along the mountain fronts of southern Arizona, are suspected of providing the pathways up which the warm waters rise toward the surface.

In some geothermal systems, investigators have found that hot fluids are contained in the highly fractured, deep basement rocks, rather than in the overlying volcanic or sedimentary rocks. Again, the overlying rocks serve as thermal insulation, preventing rapid dissipation of the heat energy. Additional geothermal resources may be found in very hot rocks that lack associated fluids. A hot-dry-rock site in New Mexico is being developed as a demonstration project. In this system, cold water is pumped down one well and is heated as it moves toward the second well through fractures in the hot rocks. At the second well, the hot water rises to the surface, where it is used to generate electricity. Such hot-dry-rock systems may exist in Arizona.

"Identified resources" in Arizona having at least low-to-moderate-temperature geothermal potential favorable for de-

velopment are shown by triangles on Figure 7.1. These areas are
Yuma, the Papago Farms, the northern Hassayampa Plain,
Chandler, Springerville–Alpine, Clifton, Safford, and Willcox.
Figure 7.1 also shows areas (circles) where low- to moderate-
temperature resources are suspected on the basis of geologic,
geochemical, and geophysical evidence: the Phoenix metropolitan area, Coolidge, Tucson, Casa Grande, San Bernardino
Valley, Flagstaff, Tonopah, and Hyder Valley. Although data
are sparse in many parts of Arizona, it is not unreasonable to
expect that on-going exploration will identify numerous additional geothermal resources in the state.

Arizona is one of eleven western states having identified
geothermal resources; however, surface manifestations in
Arizona such as hot wells and springs indicate that temperatures
are only moderately high compared to those in some other
states. Therefore, exploration companies, which understand the
risks and profits of drilling for gas, oil, and geothermal, are
concentrating on the states with potential high-temperature resources suitable for generating electricity, mainly California,
Nevada, Utah, and New Mexico.

Geothermal Drilling and Leasing

Major exploration companies have leases and lease applications in Arizona, but little geothermal drilling has been carried
out to date. Three deep geothermal test wells were drilled in
Arizona in the early 1970s, with limited success. Two of these
wells were drilled near Chandler in 1973 by Geothermal Kinetics
Systems, Inc. (GKI). Total depths were 2,807 m (9,200 feet) and
3,197 m (10,500 feet); bottom-hole temperatures in both wells
are reported to have somewhat exceeded 150°C (302°F). Amax
Exploration, Inc. and GKI drilled the third well near Eloy in
1974. Maximum depth was 2,440 m (8,000 feet); the bottom-
hole temperature was reported to be 120°C (248°F).[4] In 1980,
Phillips Petroleum, Salt Lake City, drilled six shallow gradient
holes near Clifton, and Union Oil Co. drilled one gradient hole
to 215 m (715 ft.) in the San Bernardino Valley. All of these
efforts have concentrated on locating high temperatures suitable
for electrical generation.

As of May 1, 1981, the Bureau of Land Management (BLM)
had leased a total of 21,541 acres of federal land in Arizona for
geothermal development. The Arizona State Land Department
had leased an additional 34,356 acres of state land for geothermal development. Numerous lease applications for geothermal
development were pending approval by the U.S. Forest Service,
BLM, and State Land Department as of late 1981.

Direct-Use Technology

The direct use of geothermal energy is the use of natural hot water in a given process without conversion to an intermediate energy type. The utilization of natural hot water is similar to the use of hot water heated in a boiler. Geothermal engineering design is based on information that is currently understood, and no major research advances or scientific discoveries are required. For these reasons, direct use of geothermal energy in Arizona is considered to be an immediately available energy alternative.

Most direct-use geothermal applications in Arizona will require three major components: production and injection equipment; piping systems; and heat exchangers. In addition, corrosion and scaling factors present problems in materials selection that may be unique to each geothermal application.

Production and Injection Equipment

Most geothermal uses in Arizona will require pumping equipment to control the flow of geothermal fluid. In many cases, geothermal wells flow by themselves as a result of gases present in the reservoir, because the system is artesian, or because the geothermal fluid is allowed to flash to steam as pressure is released. Under all circumstances it is advantageous to pump such self-flowing holes in order to maintain pressure in the well, and to control flashing and associated scaling.

Two types of pumps have been effectively used in geothermal development: the vertical-turbine pump, which has been used for many years in domestic and irrigation-water supply applications, and the downhole or electric submersible pump. Submersible pumps offer several advantages over vertical-turbine pumps; they deliver a larger amount of horsepower at the pump; conventional designs can operate in temperatures up to 150°C (300°F); surface requirements are minimal; the pump and motor noises are confined to the well.

Piping Systems

Once the geothermal fluid is pumped to the surface, it becomes necessary to pipe the fluid to a user site. Piping geothermal water is similar to piping any other water. The only difference is that care must be taken to prevent oxygen, the major cause of corrosion, from entering the piping system. Black steel piping is the most commonly used material. Other types of metallic pipe include copper, brass, stainless steel, and other more exotic metals. Several types of nonmetallic pipe are also commercially available, such as asbestos, cement, and plastic pipes (PVC, CPVC, Fiberglas, polypropylene, and other thermoplastic materials). With proper pipe insulation, heat loss can be reduced to around 0.1°C/km (0.3°F/mile), at a cost of less than $82 per meter ($25 per foot), using 21 cm (8 inch) -diameter pipe.[5] Today, 21 km (13 miles) is the farthest distance geothermal fluid is piped.

Heat Exchangers

Heat exchangers are another type of equipment commonly used in geothermal applications. The principal reason for having heat exchangers in geothermal systems is to confine the geothermal waters with their inherent impurities to locations where corrosion and scaling can either be controlled by materials selection, or where equipment cleaning or replacement is relatively easy. Several types of heat exchangers are commercially available. These include down-hole, shell-and-tube, flat plate, fluidized bed, direct-contact and plastic-tube heat exchangers.

Materials Selection

Corrosion, scaling, and materials selection are technological problems that must be dealt with in a geothermal system. Chemicals and elements such as oxygen, hydrogen sulfide, carbon dioxide, ammonia, hydrogen, sulfates, and chlorides are principally responsible for corrosion. Scaling is caused principally by silicates, carbonates, sulfides, and oxides.

Corrosion problems can be dealt with in two ways. Corrosion inhibitors can be added to the geothermal fluids but are often impractical owing to the large scale of the geothermal applications and to the fact that the Environmental Protection Agency (EPA) requires corrosion inhibitors to be removed from the fluid prior to disposal. Corrosion problems, therefore, are dealt with more effectively through materials selection. Scaling-control chemicals are subject to less EPA regulation. Scaling-control chemicals fall into two general classes: those that modify surface characteristics of equipment and retard nucleation and those that change the chemical character of the scale deposits.

Other Technologies

Other technologies usually associated with direct-use geothermal applications, particularly space heating and cooling applications, include forced-air fan units, convection circulation units, hydronic radiant floor or ceiling panels, heat pumps, and absorption refrigeration units. All of these devices are available as off-the-shelf commercial items. Of most interest to Arizona are the heat pump and the absorption refrigerator.

A heat pump is a machine capable of transferring heat from a low-temperature source to a higher-temperature medium. In a conventional residential furnace unit, hot air between 38°–60°C (100–140°F) is added to a colder room to maintain a desired temperature. By contrast, a heat pump is capable of absorbing heat from a 16°–33°C (60°–90°F) geothermal resource and transferring it to provide 38°–60°C (100°–140°F) air temperatures. Low temperature geothermal resources, such as have been found in Arizona, are ideal for heat pump applications.

Although heat pumps require electrical input, two to four units of heat energy are transferred for each unit of electrical energy used. In other words, one kwh of electricity supplied to a heat pump could produce from two to four kwh of equivalent electrical heat. Of greater interest to Arizona, heat pumps can be reversed to provide air cooling. Using the same principles stated above, heat from a cooler room can be pumped to a higher-temperature geothermal fluid. In this case the room gets cooler while the geothermal fluid increases in temperature. Heat pumps with reversible valves, which provide heating and cooling, are commercially available for both small-scale and large-scale applications.

Several economic advantages can be cited for using heat pumps. First, although heat pumps require a larger capital investment, annual energy costs are currently less than those incurred using conventional forced-air heating systems.[6] Second, if the heat pump is reversible, space cooling becomes possible without any additional equipment expense. Third, as fuel rates continue to escalate, the operating energy cost of using a heat pump will increase less than that of conventional equipment.

Moderate-temperature geothermal fluids can also be used in absorption refrigeration to provide space cooling. This method relies on two basic principles. First, the boiling point of water decreases as pressure decreases. Second, solutions of lithium bromide and water are able to absorb water vapor. Geothermal heat can be used to boil a diluted solution of lithium bromide and water; the resulting water vapor is then drawn to a condenser section where it is cooled and condensed. The liquid (refrigerant) then flows into an evaporator section in which pressure is low. There the refrigerant is sprayed over tubes containing water warmed by the air to be cooled. The heat removed from the water causes the refrigerant to vaporize. This vapor is then drawn to an absorber section where it is absorbed by a lithium bromide solution. The heat of absorption released when the vapor returns to a liquid state is removed by cooling water which flows through the section in a tube. The process results in a cooler temperature in the space being conditioned.

Absorption refrigeration units are commercially available items from several major air conditioning companies. Sizes range from small, suitable for individual households to large, suitable for commercial or industrial facilities. Since World War

II, most absorption refrigeration machines use hot water from boilers fired by natural gas, oil, or coal. Older absorption machines required input temperatures of 150°C (300°F). Today, absorption refrigeration machines can operate on input temperatures as low as 71°C (160°F). Research into new types of absorption solutions could result in further reductions.

Uses for Geothermal Energy

The most well-known and easily accepted concept for using geothermal resources is the generation of electricity. Two types of geothermal systems are used to generate electricity. The most desirable is a vapor-dominated system, consisting of dry steam. A less desirable but more common type of resource is the high-temperature mixture of hot water and steam. Although Arizona is not expected to have high enough temperatures for either type of system, neighboring states (California, Nevada, Utah, and New Mexico) may come to rely quite substantially on future electrical supplies generated from geothermal resources. Nearby reliance on electricity from geothermal resources may have regional impacts on Arizona.

The only developed geothermal field currently generating electricity in the United States is The Geysers, in northern California. Pacific Gas and Electric Company is generating over 900 megawatts of electricity from vapor-dominated geothermal reserves. Current estimates suggest an additional 1,441 megawatts of capacity by 1990.* A second major geothermal development site is the Imperial Valley of southern California. Currently, a 10-megawatt binary-cycle demonstration facility and a 10-megawatt flash-steam facility are in operation. Future development plans for Imperial County, including flash and binary plants, may reach 3,000 megawatts by the year 2000. Other states with plans for generating electricity from geothermal resources are Nevada, Utah, Hawaii, and New Mexico.

District Heating and Cooling

A district heating and cooling system is a network of pipes connected to energy consumers, which provides heating, cooling, hot water, or any combination of these. An analogous system is a present-day water distribution or natural gas distribution system. The major differences consist of the product being piped and limitations on distance. In the case of geothermal district systems, hot or cold water replaces natural gas or electricity as the primary source of energy for residential heating or cooling.

---

*The 1990 total would be equivalent to 9.5 percent of electric generating capacity in Arizona.

Operational district heating systems in the United States are limited, but Klamath Falls, Oregon and Boise, Idaho both rely on geothermal energy for space heating. The Oregon Institute of Technology campus in Klamath Falls is completely heated with geothermal energy, and a geothermal cooling system has been added. Furthermore, plans have been completed for extending the heating district to include fourteen government buildings in the downtown area. Similarly, in 1980, 250 residents in Boise, Idaho derived their home heat solely from geothermal energy, and the waiting list of new customers numbered 350.[7] Plans have been made in Boise to convert twelve large public buildings to geothermal heating for base-load needs. In all, the project entails supplying approximately 40 million Btu/hr of geothermal heat to over 1,000,000 square feet of office and retail space, with a current value cost savings in excess of $1 million.[8]

Principal cost components of a direct-use system are the well drilling and completion costs, transmission costs, and distribution costs. The main variable in well drilling costs is the amount of soft versus hard rock encountered while drilling. Wells drilled to 610–916 m (2000–3000 feet) can be drilled with conventional water well drilling equipment; however, deeper wells normally require larger and more expensive oil field drilling rigs. The cost of transporting the geothermal fluid depends heavily on the type of piping material used and how the pipe network is housed. Distribution costs depend mainly on the density of the population served by the geothermal system.

Of the three major components, the distribution system is typically the most costly. As a result, energy density becomes very significant in district heating and cooling systems. Energy density is usually expressed as the energy demand in a user location divided by the area. As Table 7.1 shows, the feasibility of a district system increases as energy density increases.

Table 7.1   *Economic Prospects for District Systems*

Peak Heat Density Mill. Btu/hr/acre	Area	Category
>0.97	Downtown: high-rise	very favorable
0.97-0.70	Downtown multi-storied building	favorable
0.70-0.28	City core: commercial building & multi-family apartments	possible
0.28-0.17	Residential: multi-family	questionable
<0.17	One-family house	not possible

Source: Swedish District Heating Workshop, *District Heating, Swedish District Heating Manual.* Chicago, Swedish Trade Office, 1978, p. 7.

Of concern to Arizona is the possibility of district heating and cooling systems for communities or business districts within the state. District heating systems have been shown to be feasible with resource temperatures as low as 60°C (140°F) in places such as Oregon. Cooling systems currently require resource temperatures of 105°C (220°F) to 120°C (250°F). As of 1981, only one such resource had been identified in Arizona, at Clifton, but it would not be unreasonable to expect other moderate-temperature resources to be found at depths greater than 1220 m (4000 ft) in major growth areas, such as Mesa and west Phoenix.

Studies have been performed to determine the economic viability of all potential resource sites in Arizona. These studies provide a priority list for development, define a price of geothermal heat that a user would have to pay and identify a time frame when a geothermal resource becomes economic compared to the least-cost available energy alternative. Study results have been confined to district space heating for all energy users in communities co-located with a geothermal resource, and to process heat for industrial users. Furthermore, the studies assume geothermal energy development three years after a calculated geothermal price is found to be less than the lowest-cost available alternative energy in a given area. For reference purposes, Table 7.2 presents 1981 energy prices in the Tucson area.

Table 7.2   *Energy Prices in the Tucson Area*

Type of Fuel	Cost (1981)	$/MBtu	Increases to 1990	Increases 1990–2000
Natural gas				
(residential)[2]	$ .0044/cubic foot	$ 4.44	19%	10.5%
Diesel oil	.95/gallon	7.02	12%	9.0%
Electricity				
(residential)[3]	.06/kwh	17.58	12%	7.5%
Coal (delivered)[4]	35.00/ton	1.50	10%	7.5%

[1] Based on forecast by Data Resources, Inc.
[2] Based on average residential consumption in the Tucson area.
[3] Based on Arizona Public Service Co. and Tucson Electric Power Co. rate schedules for 1200 kwh/month in summer.
[4] Based on Peabody Coal Co. price quotes.

Note: Electricity price increases result principally from increases in fuel, labor and tax. In Arizona, large increases are expected in the 1980s as a result of the construction of new plants, but large increases are not expected in the 1990s because excess capacity will exist.

Low and high policy cases are considered for two different types of developers. The policy cases were chosen in order to measure the effect of government support in bringing about near-term geothermal development. Assumptions necessary for the two policy cases are:

	Conservative Policy Case	Optimistic Policy Case
Government financial assistance, research	0	10%
Government financial assistance, development	0	25%
Production well success ratio	50%	80%
Investor rate of return (constant dollars)	25%	10%
Surface exploration cost (per site)	$500,000	0
Tax credits	0	15%
Bond rate (above inflation)	2%	2%
Conventional fuel price increase (above inflation)	4%	4%
Depletion allowance	15%	15%

In addition to the two policy cases, two types of developers are considered, one a private developer, the other a city or municipality that provides a utility service. Typically, municipal development is a more favorable case because municipalities can raise capital at lower interest rates and municipalities have a lower required return on investment.

Results for the low policy case suggest that if the district heating system is developed by private business, geothermal energy for three cities (Douglas, Goodyear, San Manuel) would be economic before the year 2000. Significant growth in the quantity of economic geothermal heat on line begins in 1994 and increases through 2000 and beyond. The economic district heating potential for the year 2000 is estimated to be 1.12 trillion Btu/year. Industrial energy supply potential begins in 1995, and 2.39 trillion Btu/year of heat energy could be supplied by the year 2000. This would represent 2 percent of Arizona's total energy consumption, using Case B assumptions.

With the city as the developer for the low policy case, economic district heat on line becomes economical for additional locations. Major development begins in 1983 and rises steadily through the year 2000. The economic heat potential for the year 2000 under city development is estimated to be 30.2 trillion Btu-year and accounts only for the residential/commercial space heat sector. By adding in private sector development by industry, geothermal energy could supply about 55 trillion Btu/year, or 4.5 percent of Arizona's total energy consumption.

The high policy case is much more optimistic for geothermal development. With private development, 83 sites have been found to be economical by the year 2000, and under city development, 98 sites. Major growth under the high case has been found to begin in 1984 under private development and 1983 under city development, and by the year 2000 private development would supply 38.1 trillion Btu/year and city development would supply 47.0 trillion Btu/year. Also, private development would supply an additional 61.3 trillion Btu/year in industrial process heat to industries co-located with geothermal resources. Principal cities found to be prospects for city and industrial development before 1985 include Douglas, Goodyear, Chandler and Chandler Heights, Coolidge, Bowie, Willcox, Litchfield Park, Glendale, Mesa, Safford, Clifton, Tucson, and Phoenix. Total geothermal use in the state, under these assumptions, would be 146.4 trillion Btu/year, or 12 percent of all energy consumption in 2000.

Several qualifications must be made with regard to the use of these data. First, the data are most useful for comparing the effect of government policy on geothermal development rather than as strict development scenarios. Second, useful comparisons can also be made between private development and city development. Third, these data do not suggest that development will be economic in any given year nor do they reflect all available resource information. Rather, they provide a relative ranking for resource sites in Arizona in terms of their economic viability and user potential.

Clearly, space heating is not the only concern within Arizona. Space cooling consumes much more energy at greater expense to energy users. In addition, the ability to use geothermal energy for cooling and heating increases resource utilization and improves overall system economics. Efforts are continuing to further evaluate the economics of space cooling using geothermal energy. Only two analyses had been performed as of 1981, one on a residential district and one on an industrial facility, both in Phoenix. The preliminary results of the analysis indicate that residential cooling is infeasible largely because of the low energy-use density. The larger industrial facility, on the other hand, had a calculated payout of 3.9 years when fast amortization was allowed. Furthermore, electricity prices today are

72 percent greater than they were when the analysis was performed. Based on preliminary data, further economic analyses are being carried out to better define the economics of geothermal space cooling systems in Arizona.

Industrial Applications

Many industrial processes require heat at temperatures less than 150°C (300°F) and could in many instances utilize local geothermal resources for these low-temperature needs. Basic industrial processes found to be adaptable to geothermal utilization include preheating, washing, blanching, peeling, evaporating, sterilizing, distilling and separating, and drying. However, in each case, the industry must be located on or near a usable geothermal resource.

Several Arizona industries, such as cottonseed oil, copper, bottling, and concrete, have been found to be located aside or near potentially usable geothermal resources, and many of these industries' production processes, from seed conditioning in the case of cottonseed oil to mixing in the case of concrete, may be accomplished through the use of geothermal energy. The five major low-to-moderate industrial energy consumers in the state are estimated to consume over 6.3 trillion Btu annually; the total low-temperature industrial process-heat market in Arizona is estimated to be 8.9 trillion Btu per annum.[9]

Agricultural and Agribusiness Applications

Agricultural applications and agribusiness operations offer a vast market for the utilization of geothermal energy. Agricultural growth applications include greenhousing, animal husbandry, aquaculture, soil warming, mushroom raising, and biogas generation. Each of these agricultural applications has been extensively documented for its integration with geothermal energy. Agribusiness applications include potential geothermal uses for food processing, sugar-beet processing, potato processing, crop drying, and slaughter operations. All of these activities require temperatures below 92°C (200°F) and are considered to be good candidates for geothermal energy utilization.

In addition, four uses of geothermal fluid have been proposed which may have the effect of conserving potable groundwater. First, increased greenhousing in Arizona could substantially reduce agricultural water consumption through more efficient water application techniques. Low-temperature geothermal energy could provide low-cost heat needed for year round greenhouse production and assist in preserving the productivity of Arizona agriculture. Second, it is possible to mix geothermal fluids with potable groundwater prior to irrigation. The effect would be to reduce potable groundwater consumption if such a practice were adopted. Preliminary investigations suggest that a mixture of certain geofluids with fresh water would be possible without significant deleterious effects to crops or soil. Third, salt-tolerant crops, halophytes, may be able to use saline geothermal waters directly, reducing groundwater requirements. Lastly, increased phycoculture, or the growing of single-cell algae for food or fuel needs, may be able to utilize hypersaline geothermal brines which currently pose expensive disposal problems in some areas. In summary, the use of saline geothermal brines in agricultural production could aid in improving the economics of a geothermal utilization scheme by reducing disposal costs, aid in conserving potable groundwater, and provide a necessary ingredient to proposed halophyte production and phycoculture in Arizona.

While major geothermal energy development in Arizona will begin in the 1990s, significant direct use development has been occurring in other western states. By 1980, there were 187 users of geothermal energy direct heat in the western United States, providing 1.487 billion Btu/year of heat. Investment in these projects totalled $5,442,000 as of September 1980. Seventy percent of the capital was provided by the federal government and 27 percent by the private sector. The remaining three percent was provided by state and local governments. Geothermal direct uses on line include space conditioning, district heating, vegetable dehydration, aquaculture, fish farming, and greenhousing.

Significant Factors Affecting Geothermal Development in Arizona

Beyond the utilization of geothermal energy and the technology associated with those uses, other factors must be addressed to complete the picture of geothermal energy as a viable energy alternative for Arizona. Other factors that will significantly affect geothermal development in Arizona include the political and legal climate, environmental impacts and mitigating techniques, and less obvious social and economic aspects as they relate to Arizona. Within each category both positive and negative aspects can be cited. These factors must be viewed as an integral part of a much broader energy policy, which offers a finite number of alternatives.

Legal

As of 1981, Arizona had only one piece of geothermal legislation, which was passed in 1977. The bill was patterned after the 1970 Federal Geothermal Steam Act. The Arizona act contains provisions for leasing of state lands and taxation of geothermal property. It also defines "geothermal resources," addresses applicability of state water laws, and amends other laws to conform with the geothermal legislation. In all, the act succeeds in laying the groundwork for the development of geothermal resources in Arizona by allowing state agencies to promulgate rules and regulations necessary for gaining access to the resource and rights to develop and utilize the resource. Unfortunately, much of the initial legislation was aimed at regulating electrical generation, a matter of small concern in Arizona because of the low grade of geothermal energy in the state.

Defining and regulating a geothermal resource, which is a direct source of energy and which must be treated differently from other types of energy and from groundwater, is a complex issue that has not yet been resolved. It is within this context that three distinct legislative barriers arise. First, recent passage of the Groundwater Management Act, and associated provisions designating Active Management Areas (AMAs), may prevent development of geothermal resources in the AMAs. Although geothermal legislation in Arizona provides exemptions from groundwater laws, the language of the Groundwater Management Act is sufficiently vague, and contains significant qualifications, that the exemption becomes a matter of interpretation. Such ambiguities remove certainty from current geothermal legislation.

Second, persons who develop geothermal energy on state land are required by state constitutional law to pay a 12.5 percent royalty rate based on the value of the product being produced from the land. For most mineral and energy resources, royalty payments are based on market values, which are easily determined. However, direct utilization of geothermal resources does not have a unique, readily identifiable market value. Since no definitive rules exist for calculating royalty rates, current interpretation suggests that the energy value be set equal to the value of the energy replaced. For example, at a price of $12.00/MBtu for electricity, the royalty for replacing that electricity with geothermal energy would be $1.50/MBtu. If instead the geothermal resource value were tied to the *least* expensive energy alternative available in a given location, incentive would be provided to switch to this alternative energy source. For example, the royalty based on a natural gas price of $4.00/MBtu would be $0.50/MBtu. Furthermore, because direct-use geothermal is a low-quality energy, it can be argued that its cost should be less than other, higher quality energy sources in order to encourage its use.

Third, current tax structure in Arizona offers clear advantages to solar energy as an alternative energy source, but the laws do not offer the same advantages to geothermal energy development. It is true that existing tax laws offer geothermal developers deductions for exploration and development expenses; however, additional tax incentives for geothermal energy development, or the removal of solar tax incentives, would place geothermal energy development on more equal footing with solar energy development. If additional tax incentives are desirable, they should include property tax exemptions, rapid amortization, income tax credits, and a geothermal drilling credit. Furthermore, state level tax incentives should include cooling devices that utilize geothermal energy in conjunction with other energy sources. A well-balanced tax program could increase the pace of geothermal development in Arizona.

Environmental

Environmental impacts are another concern regarding the development of any energy source. All energy development involves some tradeoff between energy and the environment. Energy sources with controllable environmental impacts are obviously the most desirable to develop. Much experience has been gained in controlling the environmental effects of geothermal energy development. It must be realized that each geothermal resource will differ in environmental impact, based on such factors as resource temperature and depth, local topography, geologic conditions, and intended end-use. It is difficult and somewhat misleading, therefore, to generalize about all geothermal resources. However, for purposes of this discussion, some of the more common environmental impacts which have been documented at other development sites will be addressed along with accepted methods for mitigation.

Degradation of air quality because of gaseous emissions is a major concern where wet- and dry-steam geothermal resources exist. Gaseous emissions are a problem in wet- and dry-steam fields where steam is released to the atmosphere. In Arizona, where no steam is expected to be found, this should not be a problem.

Disposal of liquid and solid wastes from geothermal systems is another area of environmental concern. Because geothermal fluids can be highly saline or toxic, precautions must be taken to dispose of them safely to preclude damaging surrounding land or waters. Apart from potential agricultural uses, two disposal methods have been legally acceptable in Arizona: reinjection of the fluids into the ground, often into the same reservoir from which they were drawn, and the use of evaporation ponds. These ponds must be lined properly to prevent seepage or leakage of geothermal effluent into groundwater aquifers or onto surrounding lands. Solid wastes that arise from drilling operations and equipment maintenance are disposed of in the same manner as in all commercial drilling operations.

Subsidence and induced seismicity are also concerns during geothermal development and production. Land subsidence can occur when fluids are withdrawn from porous reservoirs, resulting in compaction of sediments or collapse of pores in the rock structure. Subsidence may be more of a problem in hot-water geothermal fields where the reservoirs often are in semi-consolidated sedimentary rocks containing pore spaces. Mitigating measures can be implemented in order to control subsidence. One option is to maintain pressure in the geothermal reservoir by reinjecting effluent. Also, subsidence can be controlled by changing the rates of production and injection.

Seismicity is sometimes felt to be a direct result of subsurface fluid and heat withdrawal or reinjection. However, in most cases, high-temperature geothermal resources and seismicity occur naturally at the same location because the same unstable geologic conditions give rise to both features. Seismicity does not appear to be a problem in low- to moderate-temperature resource areas, but monitoring devices can be installed, as they are in high-temperature areas, to be certain.

Many further studies will be required, and are in progress, to better understand all of the environmental impacts of geothermal development. However, experience suggests that most of the problems can be dealt with effectively and at reasonable cost.[10] Geothermal development has occurred in both community centers and in sensitive agricultural areas without detrimental effect. In summary, geothermal energy development as of 1981 has not presented any serious or unsolvable environmental problems.

Social and Economic

Socioeconomic effects of geothermal development can also be suggested, though documentation is sparse.[11] It is safe to suggest that significant geothermal development would create jobs for residents, both in the development and operation stages. Furthermore, the presence of geothermal resources could attract industry to Arizona, such as food and hog processing, which are currently carried on outside of the state. Development of these industries in Arizona would benefit residents with jobs and farmers with better prices for crops and livestock.

Benefits from geothermal development could also accrue to Arizona during periods of inflation. Because the major portion of geothermal energy costs is in capital investment, unit costs would tend to rise relatively slowly, once the facilities were in place. In this respect, geothermal plants resemble other capital-intensive electric generating plants, e.g., nuclear power plants, and have a distinct advantage over energy sources subject to strong upward cost pressures, e.g., oil and gas-fired plants.

Chapter 8
Biomass Fuels

Biomass fuels are combustible or fermentable materials of vegetable origin. The biomass resource base includes trees, field crops, seaweed, algae, manure, and urban and industrial waste. It constitutes an energy form that is regenerated in the course of the annual solar cycle and is thus one form of renewable resources (along with solar, wind energy, and hydropower).

Although biomass energy typically is not included in current energy tabulations (including those used in Chapter 3), it constitutes an important share of total U.S. energy consumption, some 2.7 quads or about 3.5 percent.[1] A recent technical assessment places its potential contribution by the year 2000 at between 4 and 17 quads.[2] (Most estimates of national energy consumption for the year 2000 range between 90 and 100 quads.) Much of this total, especially in a low-use case, would come from forest products, but crop residues, animal manure, and agricultural processing wastes all could become commercially significant. In addition, ethanol from biogas and other liquid hydrocarbons from grains, grasses, and aquatic plants may emerge as an important source nationally if conditions are conducive to high biomass use. Other biomass sources, such as the biofuel crops discussed in this chapter, are unlikely to play a major role until the twenty-first century.

As the wide range of future estimates implies, the growth of biomass energy in the 1980s and '90s years is subject to considerable uncertainty. One reason for this is the interdependence between biomass and food: most biogas sources can be used as foods or animal feedstocks, or they can be converted into alcohol fuels. Tradeoffs between these uses depend not only on relative prices of grain and energy, but also on technological developments and the degree of public policy support for the respective sectors. Thus, discussion of the future of biofuels can only be tentative rather than definitive.

Currently Available Resources

A number of biofuels are of special interest to Arizona. One of these is wood, the oldest fuel source known to man. Other available resources include grain, agricultural residues and wastes, and municipal solid waste. While these classes of biofuel vary in relative abundance, all are potentially exploitable sources of biomass energy.

Wood

Some 20 million acres of Arizona's total area of 73 million acres consist of woodlands and forests, most of it located in the northern and central portions of the state and at higher elevations. Two characteristics are required for forest land to become a viable source of biomass fuel: high density and a reasonable annual growth rate. Ponderosa pine forests, which run in an east–west belt across the north-central portion of the state, best fulfill this combination of conditions. Annual growth, which contains an estimated 34.7 trillion Btu (4 percent of Arizona's 1980 energy consumption), is quite fully harvested. Most of this is allocated to the allowable cut. However, substantial residues are left in forests (some 6 trillion Btu), and another 1.74 trillion Btu is available from pre-commercial thinning. There are also substantial volumes of mill residue, which the larger mills already utilize (e.g., for generating power for their own use) or sell to other users.

Total annual biomass accumulation from wood sources has been estimated at 57.1 trillion Btu,* or 7 percent of current Arizona energy consumption.[3] However, realizing this potential would require favorable economic conditions for harvesting, conversion, and marketing; development of adequate technologies for harvesting and conversion; and land management policies to prevent environmental damages. Most important, if biomass is to be harvested for energy on a sustained basis, land management planning must incorporate this objective within a comprehensive multiple-use framework.[4]

Alcohol from Grains

Grains can be readily converted into ethanol, a form of pure alcohol, which can serve as a blending stock for motor fuel or as raw material for production of a variety of chemicals. A blend of

---

*This figure does not include chaparral and shrub regions whose annual growth rate is unknown, or sources other than bolewood.

10 percent ethanol and 90 percent gasoline, known as "gasohol," is currently being distributed in several locations of the nation. It represents an attractive motor fuel on which the present stock of U.S. automobiles can operate without engine adjustment. The basic process requires a distillation column, fermentation cook tank, and boiler, at a minimum cost of $20,000. More elaborate units, including extra fermentation tanks, extra storage tanks, a new building, and automation, could run to over $250,000 for a unit producing less than 250,000 gallons of alcohol per year.[5]

Arizona's motor fuel consumption currently amounts to nearly 1.5 billion gallons a year. If ethanol were to be substituted for ten percent of the total (to produce a 90/10 mix), 150 million gallons of ethanol would be required. Assuming that 200 gallons of alcohol can be produced per acre of agricultural products,[6] about 750,000 acres, or about 60 percent of the state's total irrigated crop acreage,* would be required. In addition, it is not clear that the overall operation produces a net energy yield, though this would not be a serious drawback if wastes or low-value residues could be used as fuel.

Residues and Agricultural Wastes

The production of conventional agricultural crops for conversion into useful energy—e.g., corn or other grains into alcohol fuels—does not appear promising in Arizona, because all of these crops require large quantities of water for irrigation. However, other potential agricultural biomass sources exist: crop residues, agricultural wastes, and animal manure. Crop residue estimates range between 346,000 and 522,000 tons, with a heat content of 3.8–5.7 billion Btu. Removal, even where technically and economically feasible, would cause loss of a source of fertilizer and may raise a number of environmental problems, among them increased erosion and loss of topsoil, flow of sediments into surface waters, increased dust, decreased water retention, and depletion of nutrients. However, some beneficial effects might ensue, e.g., lower air pollution from open burning of residues.

Agricultural wastes, defined as by-products of agricultural processing, may be suitable for combustion or gasification, or for fermentation or an aerobic digestion. Some have high value as animal feed or as chemical feedstocks. On-site incineration often costs less than transportation and disposal, creating conditions for profitable use on farms.

By far the largest source of crop residues in Arizona is cotton gin trash. Its potential yield, 2.1 trillion Btu, is well in excess of

*This figure would be cut in half if double cropping proved feasible.

total energy requirements for cotton ginning. Most of these requirements are thermal and could be met by output from low-grade incinerators or low-Btu gasifiers (uses that could also be supplied by solar energy). Because of wide seasonal swings, cogeneration with sale of surplus power to utilities may be attractive for larger operations.

Citrus pulp and peel and cheese whey, which are suitable for anaerobic digestion or fermentation, could provide low quality heat necessary for liquid fuel conversion. They are available in small but not insignificant quantities in the state.

Animal wastes can be converted into biogas (methane plus carbon dioxide) through anaerobic digestion. The number of animals in Arizona slaughterhouses is relatively small; most of the yield would be from confined chickens and cattle on feed. Total yield is estimated at 4.33 billion cubic feet with a heat content of 600 Btu/ft^3, or about 2.6 trillion Btu. (Some figures run about one-third lower.) The majority of locations are in the greater Phoenix area.

Tumbleweed

Research is currently underway on the feasibility of using tumbleweed (Russian thistle) as a fuel in either log or pellet form.[7] The work is being supported by the Arizona Solar Energy Commission and the U.S. Department of Energy. This plant was introduced accidentally into the United States in 1873 mixed with flaxseed obtained from Eurasia. It spread quickly over the western part of the country because of its ability to become established on disturbed soil, its high water-use efficiency, its effective seed dissemination, and the relative freedom from diseases and insect parasites of the region.

Experiments have been carried out on idle farmland at three Arizona locations in Pima, Pinal, and Cochise counties. The Pima study involved land retired in 1976 from cotton production; the land had been plowed, burned, and imprinted in an effort to control Russian thistle. The Pinal acreage had lain fallow for several years because of the need to lift irrigation water some 600 feet, in the face of rising energy costs; it has since been planted with jojoba. The Cochise tests were on scattered plants growing in a fallow field. The heights, densities, and yields varied considerably among the three locations. Estimates of typical yields range from 1.5 tons per acre for areas receiving less than ten inches of annual rainfall to about 6 tons per acre in areas receiving intense cultivation (including irrigation).

Commercially available farm machinery was used for harvesting (cutting and windrowing with a swather). After being left to dry, the material was either baled or cubed with alfalfa harvesting equipment. It was then ground in a hammer mill and compressed into artificial fireplace logs by commercially available machinery. One company has also farmed cubed thistle into pellets with a laboratory-scale pellet mill. Logs have a density of about 68 lb/cubic foot and a caloric value of 7,000 Btu/lb. Estimated production costs of the logs range from about $38 per ton (slightly under $3.00 per million Btu) in western Arizona locations, using Colorado River water, to $66 per ton (about $5 per million Btu) on dryland in central Arizona, southern New Mexico, and west Texas. Output as of 1981 has been experimental only, and the material not available commercially, though a test market study has been planned.

Municipal Solid Waste

The volume of municipal solid waste (MSW) in Arizona averages nearly a ton per capita per year and has been increasing roughly in line with population. Disposal sites are becoming scarcer, costs of transporting solid wastes have risen, and various technologies have been demonstrated as practical. Rising energy costs are thus beginning to make MSW attractive as a source of liquid or gaseous fuels.

For the United States as a whole, potential output, not all of it economic, is estimated at 1.2 quads. The comparable figure for Arizona is 26 trillion Btu currently and as much as 43 trillion by the year 2000 (assuming no change in waste per capita). Practicable output is estimated at 13.4 trillion Btu, the bulk of it (nearly 80 percent) in the Phoenix and Tucson areas, though Flagstaff and Yuma are also potential sites.

A recent proposal spearheaded by the City of Tucson to the U.S. Department of Energy called for construction of an MSW plant to produce refuse-derived fuel (RDF) for use by a local Portland cement plant. This would have provided an attractive energy source for the customer while reducing the landfill requirements of the city. Costs of collection and separation may have required imposition of a fee (though recovery of metals could be credited against costs). In any case, government funding for such a plant will not be forthcoming because of recent reductions in federal support for conservation and renewable energy sources.

General Economic and Environmental Considerations

The United States has not emphasized the development of biomass from existing sources, primarily because the government has left the application of technologies which are known to the private sector, and most private firms have found unsubsidized investment in biomass unattractive. (This is not the case in some other regions of the globe, where interest in biomass is strong.)* But, as with other renewable energy sources, stress on biomass is likely to revive as costs of fossil fuels increase and capital costs fall from their abnormally high 1980 levels.

Even under more favorable conditions, however, a number of problems must be solved before the full potential of this resource can be realized. One is a need to match carefully plant output with demand. This is easiest, of course, where the operation is so integrated as to provide a direct use, e.g., in some farming operations. It is more complex where some or all of the output must be sold to a utility or industrial customer. In that case, the value of the biomass fuel may become critical; for example, biogas could be economical if an electric power company had a need for peak load low-to-medium Btu fuel, but not if its sole alternative were in base-load operation in competition with coal. Second, the optimal output is typically a low-Btu fuel, rather than a pipeline quality gas, so that market potential is limited to uses where a low energy-value produce can serve. Third, past experience has been predominantly with fairly large units; information for smaller projects is often inadequate for decision-making. Fourth, in many cases, the net energy (the amount obtained from an energy source over that energy required to produce the source) obtained from biomass is negative. However, in cases where biomass could displace imported fossil fuels, this issue may be subordinated to other considerations. Finally, there may be adverse environmental effects associated with biomass production. These relate mainly to collection activities within forested areas or soil erosion (by wind and water) and removal of nutrients whether in forested areas or in agricultural production areas. Air pollution effects occur either through open or controlled burning of the biomass, through fermentation gases escaping, or through auxiliary production of energy during the production process. Little evaluation of these impacts has been undertaken thus far.

Considerable discussion has centered on the use of productive farm land for energy use rather than for food or fiber production. Considerations include the balance of payments where agricultural exports currently provide a significant positive benefit; world malnutrition in relation to the ability of the U.S. to continue exporting grains; reduced reliability of forecasting

*Representatives from both industrialized and developing countries recently participated in the United Nations Conference on New and Renewable Sources of Energy, held in Nairobi, Kenya. In addition to looking for indigenous fuel sources as a substitute for high-cost imported oil, many of the poorer countries are concerned over the rapid disappearance of their forest resources. Wood represents the main fuel for developing countries, which comprise the bulk of the world's population.

food production when land may be shifted to energy production; and the cost of food when the land production base is in competition with the value of energy derived. If biomass production becomes extensive within the United States or some of the developing countries, the relationship of productive land to food or energy production may become critical. In that event, competition between biomass and other plants for cultivable land is likely to set fairly rigid limits on the total amount of biomass that can be produced from conventional sources.*

Prospects for Arizona

Of the various current biofuel sources in Arizona, wood is being most widely used, especially at higher elevations. In Flagstaff, for example, an estimated 90 percent of single-family residences burn wood in fireplaces or stoves. On average, wood accounts for an estimated two-thirds of the total heat in that city's homes (and probably for an even greater percentage in other northern Arizona towns). Demand increased by 400 percent in the five years following the 1973 energy crisis. Expected increases in the cost of natural gas may extend this trend to other areas, even though the cost of wood in the major metropolitan areas of the state is high because of their long distances from the principal forests.

The economics of producing ethanol from grain depend heavily on the price of the grain used and on plant size. For a small (60,000 gallon-per-year) plant, 1981 production costs were estimated at $2.09 per gallon with corn at $2.50 a bushel; this increases to $2.62 a gallon for corn at $4.25 a bushel. With corn at $3.00, costs would be $2.24 a gallon for the smallest unit, but would fall to $1.48 a gallon for a plant with an annual capacity of 1 million gallons and $1.28 for 3 million gallons[8] (net figures after distillers' dry grain credit of 61–71 cents per gallon). Virtually all units now in operation have benefited from generous federal subsidies in the form of investment tax credits; these have not been continued under the Reagan Administration. However, plans for a very large (5 million gallons per year) plant at Willcox, which would be Arizona's first ethanol refinery, reportedly will proceed without federal support.[9]

Costs of producing liquids from agricultural wastes are still too high to make this a competitive source, but methane production has been demonstrated as commercial by various large operators. Reliable cost data for smaller operations are not available, however, and high capital costs remain a problem.

---

*In the United States, the main contribution of biomass may well be as high-value chemical feedstocks, rather than as fuel. This also is a more long-term potential than an immediate prospect.

Use of cotton ginning residue has been successful in Texas and may spread to Arizona if markets for the surplus gas can be developed.

Processing and utilization of tumbleweed as logs or pellets is as of 1981 in the experimental stage, and final judgment on its commercial prospects must await the outcome of further studies. Assuming that the results are favorable, and particularly if dryland farming in Arizona locations proves practicable, the potential of this source could be quite significant. The major reason is that some 20 percent of Arizona's cropland (about 290,000 acres in 1974) lay fallow, and that only about one-sixth of the state's total land area estimated to be cultivable (1.2 out of about 7.5 million acres) has been farmed each year. The potential acreage available for developing a tumbleweed industry is thus very large.

Municipal solid-waste costs vary widely with local conditions, technology employed, and desired output. In Arizona, operations could become attractive as energy costs rise, especially if capital costs should fall. To cover collection and separation costs, a dumping charge may be required, even though separation provides some credits for materials that are recovered.

Potential Future Sources

Limitations of available water, and hence cultivable land, in Arizona and other arid regions have led scientists to begin investigations of alternative biofuel sources. These cover either plants which could grow on land irrigated by water of high salinity or halophytes, which thrive in saline or other brackish water ponds; thus, they would not compete with established crops for sources of irrigation water of good quality, but instead would supplement traditional agriculture. These potential energy sources differ from those previously discussed in this chapter (and elsewhere in this book) in that research is only in the early stages. Considerable time and effort will be required to answer a host of technical, economic, environmental, and other questions before their contribution to Arizona's future energy supplies can be realistically assessed. Thus, it is unlikely, even under the best of circumstances, that they will play an important role during the time span emphasized in the report.

The largest source of saline water in Arizona is the Blue Springs, which underlies a major segment of the northeastern portion of the state. It produces some 160,000 acre feet per year with a salt content of 2,500 parts per million (ppm); this exceeds the maximum salinity for most standard crops.[10] Second, a large area in Pinal, Maricopa, and Yuma counties contains ground water with salinity in the 1,000 to 3,000 ppm range, and sizeable portions above 3,000 ppm.[11] A number of smaller deposits with concentrations up to 3,000 ppm are located in eastern and southern Arizona. The projected Yuma desalination plant will treat about 100,000 acre feet of effluent per year, of which one-third, the concentrated brine fraction, is to be disposed of in the Santa Clara Slough or in specially constructed lined evaporation ponds. Finally, it is conceivable that seawater from the Gulf of California could one day be pumped into Arizona to feed a saline agricultural industry.

Energy Crops

Of Arizona's total land resource of 72.7 million acres, some 1.6 acres (2.2 percent) are classified as cropland, and some 1.2 million acres are currently irrigated. About one-half of the total acreage under cultivation is planted with cotton. Grains, hay, citrus, and vegetables follow, in that order. While as of 1981 there were no commercial facilities that convert crops into energy fuels, research is being pursued in developing especially water-efficient crops and in domesticating desert plants, which could yield energy products and high-value chemical feedstocks. One listing of such plants, which is probably far from complete, contains seventy-three names.[12] A shorter list of plants that are potentially valuable in Arizona runs to eleven entries, including such familiar types as safflower, chaparral, chicory, buffalo gourd, gopher weed, guayule, Russian thistle, and jojoba.

One ongoing Arizona research project, which has commercial support, has emphasized gopher weed (*Euphorbia lathyris*), though other plants have also been under investigation. This research program is a long-term one and the range of questions, both scientific and economic, is wide. Answers to many of the technical questions are expected to be forthcoming in the 1980s. Results have been sufficiently interesting to warrant summarizing the principal areas on which information has been sought before it can be determined whether a large-scale commercial operation would be viable.

Euphorbia lathyris and similar oil-bearing plants yield a latex-like liquid with properties similar to crude oil. In addition, they may contain high-value components, like rubber, paraffins, and lower molecular weight hydrocarbons, which raise their potential value substantially above that of most natural crudes. The liquid must be removed in an extraction plant by means of an acetone process. The minimum economic size of such an operation is estimated to require from 37,500 acres to as much as 175,200 acres, depending on yield per acre and minimum economic size of extraction plants. The lower figure is equivalent to 75 percent of the total acreage now under cultivation for all crops in Pima County; the upper figure equals 83 percent of cultivated acreage in Pinal County. Recent research has been aimed at developing plants that yield an economic output on marginally irrigated land or on land irrigated with saline or brackish water unsuitable for planting for food, feed, or fiber crops. This would avoid the problem of energy crops having to compete with cotton and other established crops for acreage and for the increasingly scarce supply of fresh water in Arizona.

At lower elevations in Arizona, *Euphorbia lathyris* may be limited to one crop annually since the crop is subject to fungal damage during the hot summer months. An extraction plant, in order to be economical, would have to operate during most of the year at, say, 80 percent of capacity, or 292 days yearly. Since the crop would be harvested within a limited time period, probably a few weeks, it would have to be baled, hauled to the extraction plant, and stored there for varying periods. Output of the extraction plant would be shipped to a refinery, where it would be used as blending agent, rather than as principal raw material. The volume available from one such extraction plant (1,200–3,600 barrels per day) is too small to warrant construction of a long-distance pipeline to an out-of-state refinery. The economics of the operation thus presuppose either that a refinery will be constructed in Arizona within a relatively short distance from the extraction plant, or that the crop will be grown at an out-of-state location near an existing oil refinery.

Environmental impacts of growing large-scale energy crops in Arizona must be taken into account. Energy crops may cause soil erosion that differs from that of other crops. Some plants cause problems in handling, e.g., skin and eye irritations, and require handlers to wear protective gear. Burning of residue and extraction plants may cause air pollution problems unless stack gas removal equipment is installed. The research program has been designed to cope with such problems by designing a completely integrated system of production and disposal in which the waste materials of one stage become an input for the next stage, for example, by returning nitrogenous effluents from fermentation to the crops as fertilizer. In any case, biofuels are likely to be relatively benign environmentally, as compared with some other energy sources (e.g., coal or shale oil).

At recent and projected levels of petroleum prices, biofuel crops are unlikely to be economical in the United States or other countries which can afford to pay for imported fuels. Indeed, researchers at the University of California at Davis estimate that even with by-product credit, a fuel price of $150–200 per barrel would be required to make *Euphorbia lathyris* a viable fuel source.[13] Thus, purely as a source of energy these crops probably will be grown first in some poorer nations which find it difficult or impossible to meet their needs for liquid fuels through imports. In Arizona, the economic basis of biofuels depends on the value of their specialized chemical components, which may average as much as three times the simple-Btu value. Thus, one aspect of the research program has been to determine prospective market outlets for specialized plant components that will provide a strong economic basis for biofuel production.

Saline Water Energy Crops

Complementary to research into land-based biofuels is the study of crops growing in saline solutions, including halophytes, i.e., plants that may be irrigated with substantially saline wastes, and algae that thrive in hypersaline brines. Culturing of these plants in an irrigation cascade that uses and recycles saline effluents promises not only the conversion of salt from a nuisance to a valuable resource, but also generation of a new energy-crop industry that can grow in symbiosis with conventional agriculture.

The initiation of large-scale halophyte agriculture, in conjunction with brackish- and saline-water phycoculture, would permit recycling of saline effluents. Furthermore, saline aquifers and surface waters, and possibly brines from geothermal heat and power generating plants, if toxicity is low, also could become new sources of irrigation water. For geothermal plants, the power that would ordinarily be required to reinject spent (cooled) brines thus would be saved. Furthermore, at the end of the cascade of water use and reuse one may plan for final stage utilization of saline effluents in salt gradient ponds that capture and store solar energy in the form of heat. Figure 8.1 illustrates the overall concept, delineated in terms of present water use and waste and in relation to new energy conversion and power production industries that will employ currently wasted water, untapped water resources, and possibly geothermal effluents.

The key plant at the hypersaline end of the cascade of irrigation water use and reuse is the alga *Dunaliella*. This tiny, single-cell, free-swimming organism, which contains photosynthetic pigments, can grow in water ranging in salinity from 15,000 ppm (half seawater) to saturated brines with salt content of more than 300,000 parts per million (ppm). *Dunaliella* occurs naturally in salt lakes and evaporation ponds around the world, including the American Southwest. This alga has been used in Israel to produce glycerol, beta carotene, and protein. It has been shown that the algae may be thermally converted to liquid fuels, and it is also likely that fermentation to alcohol will prove possible.

Dunaliella phycoculture is expected to produce at least 30 dry-weight tons of biomass per acre per year. On an energy

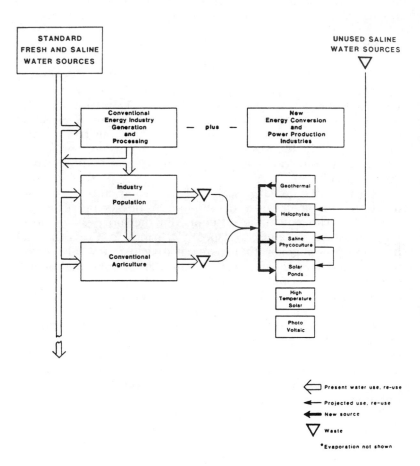

Figure 8.1   *Water Utilization Cascade*

basis, the produce of this system is equivalent to approximately 40 barrels of oil per acre per year after applying a conversion efficiency factor of 50 percent (before deducting costs of nutrients, gathering, etc). The absence of a cellulose cell wall also suggests that these plants may constitute a potential food crop. Phycoculture thus could provide chemicals, food, and fuel in temporal sequence as the scale of operations increases.

In Arizona, evaporation ponds at the Yuma desalination facility or elsewhere could be used to grow algae, and energy derived from this production could be credited against the energy cost of desalination. Saline tributaries of the Colorado River also could be used to grow algae. Colorado River Basin Water Quality Control Project piping and pumping requirements would be reduced and net energy produced. Saline effluents from geothermal energy generation plants, toxicity permitting, could be used to grow halophytes and algae, saving the energy cost of reinjection. Solar salt ponds, which may be considered as the penultimate repository of saline irrigation waters, can be used to store solar radiation as heat.

Halophyte agriculture and saline phycoculture hold the potential for production of energy as combustible biomass, oils, and fermentable alcohol feedstocks, without competing for limited supplies of fresh irrigation water. In addition, algae are naturally capable of directly fixing nitrogen. This quality offers the possibility of saving large volumes of natural gas required for the production of fertilizer.

Criteria for Future Policy

U.S. Government policy toward energy production from biomass has been criticized for a piecemeal approach that utilizes specific incentives (tax credits and subsidies) for narrowly defined programs. A variety of agencies, including the Department of Energy, the Department of Agriculture and the Solar Energy Research Institute, have been charged with developing policies and programs. The result has been a lack of overall criteria for guiding biomass development and a potential for future conflicts with other important national goals.

What appears to be required is a policy that recognizes the tradeoffs (between energy and food, fibers, etc.) and sets priorities for the use of various biomass materials. If this is to be done intelligently, a number of questions must be addressed, among them:

1. What are the full resource requirements for producing this material?
2. What is long-term productivity likely to be?

3. What are the various end uses, and what are the harvesting, handling, processing, and other requirements likely to be?
4. What are the economic and social costs involved in the production of this material?[14]

Developing answers to these questions requires a comprehensive institutional framework, a multidisciplinary approach to research, and a sufficiently long time span in which to solve technological and economic problems.

Part IV

Observations for The Future

Chapter 9

Critical Themes for
The Future

Since the early 1970s, concerns and expectations with respect to energy have changed markedly. While there is no overall energy crisis now, several factors—real and potential shortfalls of specific fuels (oil and gas), higher prices for all forms of energy, and demands for both energy and regional development that entail environmental sacrifices—have increased public awareness that it is desirable to develop long-term strategies for dealing with both our fuel and energy supply problems. Arizona's overall dependence on imported energy (primarily oil and gas), its higher-than-average population growth rate, its currently limited energy resource base, and its limited water supply, all serve to heighten the potential severity of the state's problems and to distinguish them from those of other states in the nation, including some of Arizona's western neighbors.

Yet Arizona also has opportunities. Its high degree of insolation, for example, encourages hopes of developing solar as a major energy source for the state. The state has been receptive to nuclear power, coal supplies are abundant, and some geothermal sources are distinctly possible. Less certain, if only in terms of time, are natural gas (the southern extension of the Overthrust Belt) and biomass.

Given Arizona's particular energy situation, this study has presented a range of possible energy outlooks for the year 2000, examined a number of potential supply options, and set forth some of the tradeoffs and interactions associated with any choice. Four major themes have been expressed here through varying perspectives on different energy sources and uses. They are: uncertainty, flexibility, conservation, and the interactive nature of the energy problem.

Uncertainty

Looking into Arizona's energy future, both the energy expert and the lay public face uncertainty in three areas: supply, demand, and technological change. Even for traditional fuels, it is not easy to predict how much of which fuel will be available where and when; and for the emerging fuel supply sources, the range of the estimates is so wide that, at best, upper and lower bounds can be presented. Furthermore, no fuel or energy source is completely benign, either environmentally or in terms of social (personal, governmental, and industrial) adjustments. Among fuels, the type, quantity, and location of adverse effects all vary (as does the identity of those affected), but they are ever present. At additional cost, some adverse impacts may be mitigated, but others are irreversible.

Energy prices will rise in the future not only because of efforts to make production, transport, utilization, and disposal more environmentally acceptable, but also because the cheaper sources are necessarily developed first. What is left is more expensive. If the newer sources (e.g., solar, geothermal, and biomass) cost as little now as do our current fuels, they would already be in widespread use. Subsidizing a fuel does not make it cheaper. A subsidy is simply evidence of non-commerciality: its existence indicates that the consumer is not yet paying a price that represents the full cost of all resources used at the point of consumption. A fuel subsidy may be used selectively to promote research, development, and demonstration, to offset social and environmental costs, and to provide national security protection. Wide-scale use of subsidies, however, would have serious adverse effects on the American economy and should be avoided.

Fuel cost estimates—even of traditional supplies—vary widely, and their projections even more so. This is true not only for oil and gas but also for nuclear and coal electric generating facilities. However, when compared with cost projections for other, newer energy sources, there is a difference even in the kind of projection. For the traditional fuels, one can itemize all the parts required at every stage from mine or well to consumer and on to the dump; each part can be costed. For the nearly commercial fuels (solar and perhaps geothermal), one can obtain a list of required components, but the costing is more problematic and is usually subject to needed technological developments; there may also be restrictions on the types of uses or user that make these next-generation fuels commercial. For the more distant sources (e.g., biomass), even a parts list cannot usually be generated.

The mere fact that this report presents three different but plausible scenarios shows how uncertain future demand estimates are. The reaction of consumers will be different if prices rise steadily, instead of "spiking" as a result of wars, embargoes, or other unforeseen but likely events, even if the average increase over the entire period is identical. It can be said assuredly that as energy prices rise, the rate of increase of energy demand will slow. Increases may even cease. A recession would produce the same result, as real incomes fell, leaving less disposable income for all consumer items including energy.

Conservation, land use planning, cogeneration, and distributed systems can all be viewed as examples of response from the demand side. All are fostered by high fuel prices, and all may be aided or hindered by specific subsidies (e.g., tax reductions, low-interest loans, guaranteed markets or prices) and other public action. Most current conservation is simply demand reduction due to higher prices. The adoption of conservation measures may be accelerated as a result of programs to inform and educate the public concerning currently feasible means of reducing energy consumption. Government can also aid by acting as an intervener in the market, i.e., by providing financial incentives (subsidies) and disincentives (higher fuel taxes), and by prescribing or proscribing certain developments affecting energy demand and supply. The extent of its role is partly a matter of how much time the public has available to adopt desired conservation measures, and partly a question of political philosophy.

Land-use planning, for example, is preeminently a governmental function in which energy use is but a part. Certain types of community development may be energy-efficient and therefore desirable; but such development may be opposed by others, for aesthetic or commercial reasons.

Cogeneration, widely practiced in the early part of this century, increases the value of a given quantity of fuel to the user. It has been implemented by industry, on efficiency grounds alone, as fuel prices increased. Government action could aid the market penetration of cogeneration by removing barriers to its increased development and applicability. One result of such action would be the wider use of distributed energy systems.

The linkage of Arizona's energy future to supply developments in other parts of the nation and the world complicates both the supply and demand pictures for Arizona. Yet, the answer to Arizona's uncertainties and its dependency on external circumstances is not Arizona energy self-sufficiency. Arizona cannot go it alone. That would be both prohibitively expensive and counter to the economic and political realities of our basic system of government.

Technological change, the cost of those changes, and their timing are all speculative. Engineering and agricultural breakthroughs do not necessarily occur because they are needed or because money is thrown at them to obtain a solution. Without support, whether governmental or private, solutions are even more unlikely. With respect to energy, private support usually becomes available when prices rise. The results here are speculative: higher energy prices may call forth more competing fuels and are likely to reduce demand. Where high levels of capital investment are required, the present level of interest rates is a deterring factor. If government subsidies or incentives are desired, then taxes to support the subsidies must be levied. In all of the new energy sources discussed in this book, some technological breakthrough will be necessary before they become fully competitive.

Flexibility

The elements of uncertainty make it necessary that policy choices exhibit flexibility. Policies must be capable of adjusting to changes in both external events and additions to public knowledge. Failure to allow for the possibility of a future major crisis that could disrupt supply, for example, could have severe effects on the state's economy and the lifestyles of its citizens. Thus, the time to prepare for a future emergency is during a time when traditional fuel supplies are relatively abundant.

Policies must also be flexible enough to adapt to differences in conditions and needs among local communities. Just as Arizona is different from many states in the nation, regions of Arizona differ from each other in their energy demand problems or supply options (e.g., potential for geothermal or biomass development). Similarly, while solar incidence is greatest in Arizona, given the patterns of our energy consumption, its value for heating is less here than in colder parts of the nation; current availability is greater in southern Arizona, but again, its value for space heating is higher in northern counties. This would change if or when industrial process heat applications are exploited, a cost breakthrough occurs in photovoltaic cells, solar central power stations become competitive, or solar cooling becomes economical.

There is no one answer to Arizona's energy future, and gambling on any one source is a high-risk strategy. A mix of sources, both currently available and developing, and both renewable and non-renewable, must be fully assessed if the state is to have the flexibility that an uncertain future requires. While this book has focused on three supply options (solar, geothermal, and biomass), and a demand option (cogeneration and distributed power systems), it should be reiterated that these are not the only alternatives available, and some may not prove to be the most practical for the state.

Conservation

Conservation, in our view, is not an either-or proposition, to be juxtaposed against an array of possible technological and supply choices. It is rather a critical element in all future energy scenarios.

Conservation will continue to take place naturally, as energy prices march upward. While the bulk of conservation advances to date have been price-induced and have occurred in industry, where sensitivity to costs is great, additional advances can be encouraged and achieved by direct policy action (e.g., by changes in legal codes). There is a wide variety of mechanisms that can be developed to produce even more conservation efficiencies. Some, such as tax credits, are already in existence, while others, such as mandatory energy savings, appliance efficiency ratings, and mass transit, have proven to be more controversial.

Conservation "buys" flexibility by stretching the availability of future supplies. The future energy supply requirements and the component fuels demanded are not the same in a 60-quad scenario as in a 100-quad scenario, and the development of some of the more speculative energy supply options does not become so imperative if demand is rising at a slower pace.

Changes in lifestyle will occur normally, as more conservation measures are publicly and privately implemented; most changes, however, will not be sudden. Many may be perceived as positive alterations by those affected. Perhaps more than any other aspect of the energy problem, conservation requires intense educational efforts, as citizens need to be informed of the energy-saving steps they can take and of the costs and benefits associated with those steps.

The Interactive Nature of the Energy Problem

Energy is not simply a technological problem, but also an economic, social, political, and environmental one. All of these elements interact. Approaches to Arizona's energy future cannot be taken without being affected by and affecting these elements both directly and indirectly. The development of many potential energy sources in the state, for example, cannot be separated from the question of water availability and all the environmental, socioeconomic, and political ramifications attached to that issue. Options such as photovoltaics and distributed energy systems involve a host of economic and institutional tradeoffs and interactions that pose difficulties extending far beyond their technological feasibility. Thus, the alternative options must be examined from several perspectives, and measured against other options, and against environmental, economic, and social values.

Changes are bound to come, and choices will need to be made, with efforts needed from both private and public sectors. What changes can be expected? What can be done to anticipate these changes and to become more fully aware of the options for dealing with them? What are the costs and benefits of each option, and of any given option compared to another? What can and should be done by individuals, by local communities, and by the state? The challenge ahead is open for discussion on these issues, as Arizonans prepare to move through the transition to a new energy future.

Chapter 10

Arizona Supply and Demand Constraints

The historical sources of energy in Arizona are oil, gas, and hydropower. The first two are imported from out of state; a portion of the oil supply originates overseas. Hydropower is used only for electric generation. In the future, it is unlikely to increase in availability and may even decrease in drought years. While oil and gas are currently used in a variety of sectors in Arizona, oil may come to be used chiefly as a transport fuel, while gas may be limited to residential and commercial consumption.

The use of Arizona's abundant coal is fairly recent, and coal should not be in short supply at any time during our forecast period, but it feeds only one in-state power plant; all others operate on imports from other states. Large-scale in-state coal liquefaction and gasification to produce substitutes for oil and gas are unlikely because of the required water consumption. Furthermore, gasification (common in the late 1800s and early 1900s) and liquefaction are not currently cost-competitive. Plants are highly capital intensive and would take six to ten years to build, so they are not an option for sudden emergencies. Nationally, even under the spur of higher energy prices, the mid-1990s is the earliest date that an appreciable industry could be developed. At the current rate of energy price increases it is likely to be delayed.

Although nuclear power is a current energy source, the current mining and milling of uranium, its enrichment, and fuel assembly fabrication are all done out-of-state. Its use is limited to electric power generation, but electricity has wide application. The further development of nuclear power in Arizona will depend in part on the costs of electric generation by nuclear energy versus coal generation costs. The cost of nuclear power is both economic and social and may be increased as a result of perceived issues related to plant safety and waste disposal. The location of waste disposal is a matter of current debate. Additional development could take place on the basis of electricity exports if the state views electricity exports as an important economic benefit.

Of the non-traditional fuels, solar power is already available. As of 1981, it was not fully competitive, but will likely become so in at least some applications in the future. As a source of low- to medium-temperature energy for hot water or for process heat, solar power will make the greatest present and near-term contribution. To this may be added passive solar construction in residential use. No new technology is required, but some legal barriers must be eliminated. For residential use, passive solar and flat plate collectors are almost cost-effective. They are likely to be more so in the northern counties where more heating is required than in the southern portion of the state. Application will be limited by the rate of new home construction, the age of distribution of housing, and the additional costs of retrofitting existing housing.

For commercial and industrial use, location is less important. Alternate fuel costs are the deciding factor. Flat plate and focused collectors are likely to be fully competitive with natural gas in the production of hot water and, perhaps, process heat within the next five to ten years. Central power stations are further in the future. Photovoltaics as a means to produce electricity directly from sunlight are presently so expensive that their use is limited to remote locations. If, and when, the production costs of the cells fall sharply from current levels, photovoltaics may become a significant factor in Arizona's energy balance. Estimates of when this will occur, which are highly speculative, have ranged from 1985 to 2000.

Geothermal energy in Arizona, if and when developed, is likely to be limited to low- and medium-temperature hot water. In specific locations it may compete with solar energy, natural gas, and perhaps electricity. Its use will be site-specific; the energy produced will not be transported. Geothermal will present waste disposal problems requiring specific solutions. Given the current level of exploration and drilling activity, the time necessary for development and existing limited incentives, a significant contribution from geothermal is not likely before 1990. Moreover, based on current information, the resource base in Arizona is smaller than that of other western states.

Biomass is a broad area and the parts should not be confused. The technology for the utilization of agricultural and forest wastes is currently available. Their use will be local, and Arizona does not have a great deal of either. Urban waste can be used now to generate electricity or produce gas. Recycling of metal, glass, and other material can be used as process credits, but given the low population densities of Arizona's cities, collection costs are high. Biomass farms cannot compete with traditional crops and all development efforts must be oriented toward new crops on new lands utilizing new water resources. These new water resources will of necessity be ones which are too poor in quality to be used for traditional agriculture and industry. Although technical breakthroughs may occur which will bring bioenergy on-line sooner, we do not anticipate significant contributions prior to the year 2000, the limit of our forecast.

In summary, it should be noted that none of the new fuels will replace gasoline, jet fuel, or diesel oil in transport use in Arizona on a significant scale. Residual oil and No. 2 home heating oil will be displaced, but their use in the state is small. Natural gas may be replaced by any and all of the alternative fuel options. In this, however, the alternative options are also, largely, competing against each other.

On the demand side, cogeneration and distributed energy systems are current state-of-the-art and have been so since 1910. What we see now is a revival. The limitations are mainly institutional and legal. However, large-scale cogeneration requires the type of industrial base that needs both large amounts of hot water (or process heat) and electricity (or the opportunity to sell electricity). Arizona does not have such a base and is unlikely to get one because of water limitations. The contribution of cogeneration thus will be small.

A Final Word

With the first energy crisis, in 1973–74, Arizona and the nation entered a transition period during which oil and gas are being replaced by traditional fuels in new forms and by new energy sources, some of which are renewable and environmentally acceptable. By the end of the century, the first phase of this transition, which marks the development and application of near-economical sources, may be nearly completed.

In viewing these changes, one should recall that the United States, and the western world as a whole, have gone through several similar changes before. The growth of an industrial base in the 19th century was accompanied by a shift from wood and water power to coal as the chief fuel. The first decades of the 20th century saw a great spread of electricity from homes and factories. Between 1935 and 1950, industries and residential units shifted from coal to oil and gas. In the Southwest, low-cost natural gas replaced solar energy in some uses (e.g., water heating).

Two major differences between these past transition periods and the current one stand out. One is the fact that, in all previous instances, the newer sources were cheaper, more convenient, and generally cleaner. Better alternatives were driving out established ones, so that consumers could respond to normal market incentives in a smooth, gradual adaptation. This time, the changes are being forced on unwilling consumers by higher prices and threatened supply deficiencies. Government action to lessen the adverse impact on various groups becomes a much more serious option in such circumstances.

The other difference is that past transitions were generally gradual and represented the outcome of competitive market forces. This time, however, the concentration of oil reserves in foreign, highly volatile regions, under the control of a small group of producers, greatly increases the risk of supply interruptions and sudden price jumps. The only available sources of protection against such events are a combination of storage capacity, allocation, and coupon rationing: the huge sudden price increases which market-price rationing would require may not be politically acceptable in the short run. The precise role of government on the federal, state, and local levels in minimizing the impact of supply interruptions remains to be defined.

Perhaps the overriding conclusion to emerge from this book is the need for both energy suppliers and energy users to maintain a degree of flexibility. No one can be entirely certain of how rapidly energy prices will increase, how severe and how frequent oil supply restrictions may be, what precise technological advances will emerge, and how rapidly alternative energy sources will become economical. These uncertainties are bound to increase the complexities of energy planning and decision-making. The penalties for those who fail to keep informed may be severe, but the rewards to those who adapt their decisions to changing conditions may be substantial.

Notes to the Chapters

Chapter 2

1. Morris A. Adelman et al., *No Time to Confuse* (San Francisco: Institute of Contemporary Studies, 1975).

2. U.S. Department of Energy, *1980 Annual Report to Congress,* Vol. Three (Washington: U.S. Government Printing Office, 1980), p. 124.

3. The United States has 113 billion tons of a world total of 492 billion tons of recoverable coal reserves. *See* World Energy Conference, *World Energy Resources 1985–2020* (n.p.), p. 66–67.

4. *See* National Academy of Sciences, Study of Nuclear and Alternative Energy Systems (CONAES), *U.S. Energy Supply Prospects to 2010* (Washington: U.S. Government Printing Office, 1979), p. 88.

5. *See* Richard Nehring and E. Reginald Van Driest III, *The Discovery of Significant Oil and Gas Fields in the United States* (Santa Monica, California: The Rand Corporation, 1981).

6. U.S. Department of Energy, "Securing America's Energy Future," *The National Energy Policy Plan* (July 1981), p. 9, 12.

Chapter 3

1. Paul Bracken, *Arizona Tomorrow: A Precursor of Post-Industrial America* (Croton-on-Hudson, N.Y.: Hudson Institute, 1979).

Chapter 4

1. The combined market share of the four largest gasoline marketers in 1980 was 28.5 percent. See *Lundberg Letter,* Vol. VIII, No. 8, p. 2.

2. U.S. Federal Trade Commission, "Quarterly Financial Report for Manufacturing, Mining, and Trade Corporations," in *Statistical Abstract of the United States,* various years.

3. A. D. Johanny, "OPEC and the Price of Oil: Cartelization or Alteration of Property Rights," *Journal of Economic Development* (Autumn 1979), p. 77–80.

4. "World Oil Production," *Petroleum Economist,* Jan. 1982, p. 35.

5. U.S. Department of Energy, *International Energy Indicators* (June 1980), p. 28.

6. U.S. Department of Energy, "Securing America's Energy Future," p. 28.

7. Roger Sant, *The Least-Cost Energy Strategy: Minimizing Consumer Cost Through Competition* (Arlington, Va.: The Energy Productivity Center, 1979); See also Marc Ross, "Public Policy and Efficient Use of Energy," in Gregory A. Daneke and George K. Lagassa, eds., *Energy Policy and Public Administration* (Lexington, Mass.: D.C. Heath, 1980), p. 153–164.

8. Robert Pindyck, *The Structure of World Energy Demand* (Cambridge, Mass.: MIT Press, 1979), Chapters 4–6.

9. SRI International, *California Energy Futures* (Sacramento: California Energy Commission, 1980).

10. U.S. General Accounting Office, *Electrical Energy Development in the Pacific Southwest* (Washington: U.S. General Accounting Office, 1979).

11. Office of Technology Assessment, *Residential Energy Conservation* (Washington: U.S. Government Printing Office, n.d.).

12. W. H. Cunningham and S. C. Lopreato, *Energy Use and Conservation Incentives* (New York: Paraeger, 1977); M. Savitz and Eric Hirst, "Technological Options for Improving Energy Efficiency in Residential and Commercial Building," in John Sawhill, ed., *Energy Conservation and Public Policy* (Englewood Cliffs, N.J.: Prentice-Hall, 1979); *Analysis of Institutional Mechanisms Affecting Residential and Commercial Building Retrofit* (Columbia, Md.: Hittman Associates, Sept. 1980); and *Residential Energy Conservation.*

13. Robert Stobaugh and Daniel Yergin, *Energy Future* (New York: Random House, 1979); and Hittman Associates, *Analysis of Institutional Mechanisms.*

14. See Melvin H. Chiogioji, *Industrial Energy Conservation* (New York: Marcel Dekker, 1979).

15. *Arizona Guidelines for Energy Conservation in New Buildings* (Phoenix: Arizona Energy Office, 1980).

16. *Solar Standards Seminar Workbook* (Phoenix: Arizona Solar Energy Commission, 1981).

17. *Survey of Current and Potential Home Energy Management Activities Among Homeowners in Arizona* (Phoenix: Office of Energy Programs, n.d.). Another survey of four communities in the country, one of which was Tucson, yielded similar results. See *Energy Conservation Technology Education Program: Final*

Report (Springfield, Va.: National Technology Information Service, n.d.).

18. *Ibid.*

19. National Academy of Sciences (CONAES), *Energy in Transition* (San Francisco: W. H. Freeman & Co., 1980), p. 470.

20. Helen M. Ingram et al., *A Policy Approach to Political Representation: Lessons From the Four Corners States* (Baltimore: The John Hopkins Press for Resources for the Future, 1980), p. 118.

21. Miller B. Spangler, "Risks and Psychic Costs of Alternative Energy Sources for Generating Electricity," *The Energy Journal* 2, no. 1 (Jan. 1981), p. 37–59; Comment by Daniel R. Kazmer and Reply by Spangler, *The Energy Journal* 2, no. 4 (Oct. 1981).

22. Much of this material is extracted from Ingram et al.

23. Gary D. Weatherford and Gordon C. Jacoby, "Impact of Energy Development on the Law of the Colorado River," *Natural Resources Journal* 15 (Jan. 1975), p. 171–214.

24. Arizona Department of Transportation, *Arizona Transportation Energy: Usage Patterns* (December 1977).

25. Arizona Department of Transportation, *Arizona Transportation Energy: A Case Study for the Phoenix Area in the Year 2000* (Sept. 1977), p. 46.

26. *Ibid.*, p. 24.

27. James S. Roberts, *Energy, Land Use, and Growth Policy: Implications for Metropolitan Washington* (Washington: Council of Governments, 1975).

28. Dale Keyes and George Peterson, *Metropolitan Development and Energy Consumption* (Washington: The Urban Institute, 1977).

29. Than Yan Cao and Dennis C. Cory, "Mixed Land Uses, Land-Use Externalities, and Residential Property Values: A Re-evaluation," *Annals of Regional Science*, 1982. A thorough discussion of public policy options for mixed-use development is provided by D. Procos, *Mixed Land Use: From Revival to Innovation* (Stroudsburg, Penn.: Dowden, Hutchison and Ross, 1976).

30. Robert Healy, *Land Use and the States* (Baltimore: Johns Hopkins Press, 1976).

31. U.S. Department of Energy, "Securing America's Energy Future."

32. Colin Norman, "Energy Conservation: The Debate Begins," *Science* 212 (April 24, 1981), p. 424–426.

33. This material is excerpted in part from T. English, *A Guide for Developing a Local Emergency Energy Plan* (unpublished report to the Arizona SEC, Western SUN, and Arizona League of Cities and Towns).

34. U.S. Senate Committee on Energy and Natural Resources, *The Geopolitics of Oil* (Staff Report, Nov. 1980), Chapter II.

35. "U.S. May Not Gain by Cutting Oil Imports," *The Wall Street Journal,* July 13, 1981.

Chapter 5

1. Christopher Flavin, "Energy and Architecture: The Solar and Conservation Potential," *World Watch Paper* 40 (Nov. 1980), p. 11.
2. J. F. Peck et al., *Offpeak Power Use in Passive Solar Homes* (unpublished report of the University of Arizona Environmental Research Laboratory, June 1981).
3. Flavin, p. 32.
4. Office of Management and Budget, *Standard Industrial Classification Manual* (Washington: U.S. Government Printing Office, 1972).
5. "The Business of Agriculture," *Today's Business* 4, no. 16 (Jan. 1979), p. 59.
6. Arizona Public Service Company, *Saguaro Power Plant Repowering Project Final Technical Report Conceptual Design* I, DOE/SF 10739-2 (July 1980); *Solar Central Receiver Hybrid Power System Final Technical Report Conceptual Design* II, DOE-ET-21038-1 (Sept. 1979).
7. Don Osborn, personal communication, 16 June 1981.
8. "Solar Office Works to Promote Use of Sun Energy in Arizona," *Arizona Currents* (June 1981), p. 4–5.
9. Nancy Lee Jones, "Aesthetic Restrictions and the Use of Solar Devices," *Environmental Affairs* 8 (1979), p. 33–58.
10. Osborn, personal communication.
11. *Ibid.*
12. W. C. Dickinson and P. N. Cheremisinoff, *Solar Energy Technology Handbook* (New York: Marcel Dekker, 1980).
13. Osborn, personal communication.

Chapter 6

1. See *Energy User News,* May 11, 1981.
2. John E. McConnell, "Why the Debate Over Cogeneration?" *Public Utilities Fortnightly* (Aug. 28, 1980), p. 46.
3. "Utilities Likely Will Be Told to Buy Excess Electricity," *The Arizona Republic,* July 6, 1981.
4. Ed Sherry, "Energy Interchanges Between Cogenerators and Utilities," *Public Utilities Fortnightly* (Dec. 21, 1978), p. 16.
5. "Cogeneration Advances as Energy Source," *The Wall Street Journal,* May 29, 1981.
6. *Ibid.*
7. Rocco Fazzolare et al., *Assessment of the Potential for Cogeneration in the State of Arizona,* Research Report, University of Arizona, July 1981, p. 351.

8. U.S. Federal Energy Administration, *The Potential for Cogeneration Development in Six Major Industries by 1985* (Washington: n.p., 1977).

Chapter 7

1. L. J. P. Muffler, ed., *Assessment of Geothermal Resources of the United States, 1978,* U.S. Geological Survey Circular 790, 1979, p. 49.
2. *Ibid.,* p. 56.
3. M. Ellen Hale, ed., *Arizona Energy: A Framework for Decision* (Tucson: University of Arizona Press, 1976), p. 62.
4. F. Dellechaie, "A Hydrothermal Study of the South Santa Cruz Basin Near Coolidge, Arizona," in *Proceedings of the Second United Nations Symposium on the Development and Use of Geothermal Resources* 1, 1976, p. 339–348.
5. John Lund et al., *Assessment of the Geothermal Potential Within the Bonneville Power Authority Marketing Area* (Klamath Falls, Ore.: Oregon Institute of Technology, 1980), p. 48–67.
6. *Ibid.,* p. 67.
7. Phillip J. Hanson, "Boise Geothermal District Heating, 1892–1982," unpublished typescript, 1980.
8. M. J. Pasqualetti, "The Site-Specific Nature of Geothermal Energy: Its Effects on Land-Use Planning," unpublished manuscript, 1981.
9. Don H. White et al., *Evaluation of Geothermal Energy in Arizona,* Third Quarterly Report of the Arizona Geothermal Commercialization Team (1980), p. 73–89.
10. M. J. Pasqualetti, "Geothermal Energy and the Environment: The Global Experience," in *Energy: The International Journal* 5 (1980), p. 111–165.
11. J. Pick and E. Butler, "Sociological Impact," in S. Edmunds and A. Rose, eds., *Geothermal Energy and Regional Development: The Case of Imperial County* (New York: Praeger, 1979), p. 122–161.

Chapter 8

1. J. Schnorr et al., *Biomass Feasibility Study for the State of Arizona* (Flagstaff: Northern Arizona University, 1981).
2. Office of Technology Assessment, *Energy From Biological Processes: Technical and Policy Options* (Boulder, Co.: Westview Special Studies, 1981), p. 3. The estimates do not include municipal solid waste.
3. P. F. Ffolliot, W. O. Rasmussen, and J. G. Patterson, "Biomass for Energy: Potential in Arizona," *Biosources Digest* 2, no. 4, p. 240–247.
4. *Ibid.*

5. James E. Williams, "Fuel From Farm Products," *1980 Forage and Grain Report*, University of Arizona College of Agriculture, 1981, p. 1.

6. *Ibid.*

7. Martin M. Karpiscak and Kennith E. Foster, "Tumbleweed: A Candidate for Synthetic Solid Fuels," paper presented at the U.N. Conference on Small Energy Resources, Los Angeles, Sept. 9–18, 1981.

8. S. Hathorn et al., "Some Economic Aspects of Ethanol Production," *Fuel From Farm Products*, p. 14–18.

9. "Ethanol Firm to Be Built in Willcox," *Arizona Daily Star*, Aug. 29, 1981.

10. L. R. Kister, "Quality of the Groundwater in the Lower Colorado River Region, Arizona, Nevada, New Mexico, and Utah," *Hydrological Investigations Atlas*, U.S. Geological Survey Publication HA-478 (1973).

11. E. S. Davidson, *Summary Appraisals of the Nation's Groundwater Resources: Lower Colorado Region*, Geological Survey Professional Paper 813-R (1973).

12. D. Gilpin et al., *Energy From Biological Processes, Volume III: Appendices*, cited in Schnorr, *op. cit.*, p. 3.5–3.7.

13. R. M. Sachs et al., *"Euphorbia lathyris:* A Potential Source of Petroleum-like Products," *California Agriculture*, July-Aug. 1981, p. 29–32.

14. Otto C. Doering III, "Impact of National Biomass Policy on Agriculture: What Are the Tradeoffs?" paper presented at the Special Session of the American Society of Agronomy, Crop Science Society of America, and Soil Science Society of America, Detroit, Nov. 30–Dec. 5, 1980.

Suggested Readings

Chapter 1

Arizona Bureau of Mines. *Bulletin 182, Coal, Oil, Natural Gas, Helium and Uranium in Arizona.* 1970.

de Gennaro, Nat, ed. *Arizona Statistical Abstract, A 1979 Data Handbook.* Northland Press, in cooperation with University of Arizona, 1979.

Frank, Helmut J. *Arizona Energy Inventory: 1977.* University of Arizona, February 1977.

Hale, M. Ellen, ed. *Arizona Energy: A Framework for Decision.* Tucson: University of Arizona Press, 1976.

Independent Petroleum Association of America. *The Oil Producing Industry in Your State.* 1981.

Valley National Bank. *Arizona Statistical Review.* 37th Annual Edition, September 1981.

Chapter 2

National Academy of Sciences, Study of Nuclear and Alternative Energy Systems (CONAES). *U.S. Energy Supply Prospects to 2010.* Washington: U.S. Government Printing Office, 1979.

Nehring, Richard and E. Reginald Van Driest III. *The Discovery of Significant Oil and Gas Fields in the United States.* The Rand Corporation, January 1981.

U.S. Department of Energy. *Low Energy Futures for the United States.* Washington: U.S. Government Printing Office, 1980.

———. "Securing America's Energy Future." *The National Energy Policy Plan.* July 1981.

———. *State Energy Data Report.* September 1981.

———. *1981 Annual Report to Congress,* Vol. Three. Washington: U.S. Government Printing Office.

Chapter 4

Arizona Academy. *Arizona Water: The Management of Scarcity.* Phoenix: Arizona Academy, 1977.

———. *Toward the Year 2000: Arizona's Future.* Phoenix: Arizona Academy, 1980.

Arizona Department of Transportation. *Arizona Transportation Energy: A Case Study for the Phoenix Area in the Year 2000.* Phoenix: n.p., 1977.

Hale, M. Ellen, ed. *Arizona Energy: A Framework for Decision.* Tucson: University of Arizona Press, 1976.

Ingram, Helen M. et al. *A Policy Approach to Political Representation: Lessons From the Four Corner States.* Baltimore: The Johns Hopkins Press for Resources for the Future, 1979.

Kneese, Allen V. and Blair T. Bower. *Environmental Quality and Residuals Management.* Baltimore: The Johns Hopkins Press for Resources for the Future, 1979.

Lipschutz, Ronnie D. *Radioactive Waste: Politics, Technology, and Risk.* Cambridge, Mass.: Ballinger, 1980.

Policy Studies Journal VII, Autumn 1978.

Regens, James L.; Gregory A. Daneke; and Robert W. Ryckoff, eds. *Energy Development in the West, Constraints and Opportunities.* New York: Praeger, 1982.

Sant, Roger. *The Least-Cost Energy Strategy: Minimizing Consumer Cost Through Competition.* Arlington, Va.: The Energy Productivity Center.

Spofford, Walter O., Jr. et al. *Energy Development in the Southwest: Problems of Water, Fish, and Wildlife in the Upper Colorado River Basin.* Baltimore: The Johns Hopkins Press for Resources for the Future, 1980.

SRI International. *California Energy Futures.* Sacramento: California Energy Commission, 1980.

U.S. General Accounting Office. *Electrical Energy Development in the Pacific Southwest.* Washington: U.S. General Accounting Office, 1979.

Chapter 5

Dickinson, W. C. and P. N. Cheremisinoff. *Solar Energy Technology Handbook.* New York: Marcel Dekker, 1980.

Energy Management and Policy Analysis Group, University of Arizona. "Survey and Analysis of Solar Energy Process Heat Opportunities in Arizona." Report of the Engineering Experiment Station, University of Arizona, 1979.

Kreith, Frank and Jan F. Krider. *Principles of Solar Engineering.* New York: McGraw-Hill, 1978.

Meinel, Aden B. and Marjorie P. Meinel. *Applied Solar Energy, An Introduction.* Reading, Mass.: Addison-Wesley, 1976.

Solar Energy Research Facility, University of Arizona. *A Guidebook for Solar Process Heat Applications.* Phoenix: Arizona Solar Energy Commission, 1981.

Chapter 6

Fazzolare, Rocco et al. *Assessment of the Potential for Cogeneration in the State of Arizona.* Tucson: University of Arizona, July 1981.

U.S. Federal Energy Administration. *The Potential for Cogeneration Development in Six Major Industries by 1985.* Prepared by Resources Planning Associates, 1977.

Chapter 7

Anderson, D. N. and J. W. Lund, eds. *Direct Utilization of Geothermal Energy: A Technical Handbook.* Klamath Falls, Ore.: Oregon Institute of Technology, 1979.

Collie, M. J. *Geothermal Energy: Recent Developments.* n.p.: Noyes Data Corporation, 1978.

Di Pippo, R. *Geothermal Energy as A Source of Electricity.* Washington: U.S. Department of Energy, 1980.

"Geothermal Resources in Arizona: A Bibliography (1867–1981)." Tucson: Arizona Bureau of Geology and Mineral Technology, 1982.

Kruger, P. and C. Otto, eds. *Geothermal Energy: Resources, Production, Stimulation.* Stanford: Stanford University Press, 1973.

Wahl, E. F. *Geothermal Energy Utilization.* New York: John Wiley and Sons, 1977.

Chapter 8

Campos-Lopez, Enrique et al. *Renewable Resources: A Systematic Approach.* New York: Academic Press, 1980.

Office of Technology Assessment, U.S. Congress. *Energy From Biological Processes: Technical and Policy Options.* Boulder, Co.: Westview, 1981.

Sacks, Roy M. et al. "*Euphorbia lathyris:* A Potential Source of Petroleum-like Products." *California Agriculture* (July–Aug. 1981).

Schnorr, Janet K. et al. *Biomass Feasibility Study for the State of Arizona.* Flagstaff: Northern Arizona University, 1980.

University of Arizona, College of Agriculture. "Fuel From Farm Products." Reprinted from *1980 Forage and Grain Report.* Tucson: University of Arizona, 1980.

Index